PARENTAL GUIDANCE
ADVISED

PARENTAL GUIDANCE
ADVISED

Adult Preaching from the Old Testament

Edited by

Alyce M. McKenzie

and

Charles L. Aaron Jr

CHALICE
PRESS

ST. LOUIS, MISSOURI

Cover art: iStock & depositphots.com
Cover design: Scribe, Inc.

www.chalicepress.com

Print: 9780827230477   EPUB: 9780827230484   EPDF: 9780827230491

**Library of Congress Cataloging-in-Publication Data
available upon request**

Contents

JOHN C. HOLBERT

Tribute to John C. Holbert

John Holbert, in whose honor these essays are offered, grew up in Phoenix, Arizona, and attended Grinnell College. He enjoyed singing, and in his teens developed a striking tenor voice, which is called a "Heldentenor." He began as a student at Perkins School of Theology of Southern Methodist University (SMU) in 1968. He finished his Ph.D. in Hebrew Bible there in 1974, under the able tutelage of W. J. A. Power. After two years as an associate pastor in Lake Charles, Louisiana, John returned to academic life, teaching courses in Hebrew and Hebrew Bible at Texas Wesleyan College (now Texas Wesleyan University) in Fort Worth and then at Perkins School of Theology. From 1981–1984 he directed both the Doctor of Ministry program and the program of Continuing Education at Perkins. In 1984 John became Assistant Professor of Homiletics at Perkins, and in 1995 he was awarded the Lois Craddock Perkins Chair in Homiletics, from which he retired in 2012.

John's partner in life is the multigifted Rev. Dr. Diana Holbert, herself recently retired from the United Methodist ministry. They have two adult children, Sarah and Darius.

This collection of essays on preaching the Old Testament honors the central passion of John's academic and ecclesial life and his contribution to the preaching and teaching ministries of so many seminary students, pastors, and lay persons across the years. From 1984 to 2012 John taught 60 sections of Introduction to Preaching at Perkins. That means he influenced 800 students and listened to at least 3,500 sermons. His excellence in teaching has been recognized by both students and faculty colleagues alike. In 1989 he received the Marguereta Deschner teaching award for "outstanding teaching that reflects a special awareness and appreciation for the presence of women in academic endeavors." He was honored with an Altshuler Distinguished Teaching Award in 2005. He has been a mentor and encourager to both students and faculty colleagues. He was the reason Charles Aaron, one of the editors of this volume, pursued a Ph.D. in Old Testament and continues to teach and write in this area. He has been a valued friend, mentor, and guide to the other editor of this volume, Alyce McKenzie, since she joined the homiletics faculty at Perkins 13 years ago.

John's influence has not been limited to teaching future pastors in Perkins classrooms. He has led countless preaching and biblical workshops for pastors and lay persons alike. Over the years he has developed a loyal following among United Methodist church folk in North Texas. There, they don't care what the topic is as long as John Holbert is the teacher! Since his ordination as a United Methodist elder in 1976, John has taught and preached in over 1,000 churches in 40 states and in 15 countries. He has served two interim pastorates, bringing leadership to difficult situations at First United Methodist Church of Fort Worth in 1994 and at FUMC of Dallas in 1997.

Far more than once, someone has come up to John after a sermon or talk and said, "Your voice is so beautiful; I could listen to you read the phone book." John has used his vocal talents in the community, recording audio books for the blind (most recently a 720-page biography of Mark Twain) and singing oratorios in churches and concert venues around the Dallas/Fort Worth Metroplex.

John is the author of 10 books and many articles in both scholarly and professional journals. His focus is on preaching the Old Testament, particularly the narrative portions and the book of Job. In recent years he has turned his interest to preaching and environmental concerns. His new book on storytelling in preaching, Telling the Whole Story, was published in the summer of 2013. He has completed a novel on King Saul and is working on a sequel on King David. John is the author of a weekly column entitled "Opening the Old Testament," hosted by the website Patheos.com that draws over 15,000 readers a month.

John and Diana's travel has taken them to visit Spain, Alaska, England, and the Mediterranean. He has lectured on seven cruises with Educational Opportunities, and is scheduled to do more of these events in the future. We won't go into anymore detail concerning these travels lest you become jealous. But these trips are part pure fun, part teaching, and part research.

We, the co-editors of this volume, cannot imagine a more congenial, supportive, trustworthy, and delightful colleague than John C. Holbert. We deeply appreciate his friendship and look forward to many more years of collaboration and friendship.

It is our hope that this volume of essays on preaching and teaching the Old Testament by John's friends and colleagues will fire the imagination, nourish the intellect, and energize the soul of those who read them. Much like the Old Testament itself and like John himself, as one who continues to labor in its vineyards.

Alyce M. McKenzie and Charles Aaron

Works by John C. Holbert

Books

1991 *Preaching Old Testament* (Nashville: Abingdon Press, 1991).

1991 *A Storyteller's Companion to Genesis*, with Michael Williams (Nashville: Abingdon Press, 1991).

1992 *Psalms for Praise and Worship*, with S. T. Kimbrough, Jr., and Carlton R. Young (Nashville: Abingdon Press, 1992).

1995 *Holy Root, Holy Branches*, with Ronald J. Allen (Nashville: Abingdon Press, 1995).

1999 *Preaching Job* (St. Louis: Chalice Press, 1999; republished by Wipf & Stock, 2011).

2002 *The Ten Commandments: A Preaching Commentary* (Nashville: Abingdon Press, 2002.)

2011 *What Not to Say*, with Alyce M. McKenzie (Louisville: Westminster John Knox Press, 2011).

2011 *Preaching Creation* (Eugene, OR: Cascade, 2011).

2013 *Telling the Whole Story: Reading and Preaching Old Testament Stories* (Eugene, OR: Cascade, 2013).

Articles

1981 "The Skies Will Uncover His Iniquity: Satire in the Second Speech of Zophar (Job 20)," *Vetus Testamentum*, XXXI, 2 (1981) 171–179.

1981 "Deliverance Belongs to Yahweh! Satire in the Book of Jonah," *Journal for the Study of the Old Testament* 21, 1981, 59–81. Reprinted in *The Prophets*, ed. Phillip R. Davies (Sheffield, England: Sheffield Academic Press, 1996), 334–354.

1983 "The Rehabilitation of the Sinner: The Function of Job 29–31," *Zeitschrift für die alttestamentliche Wissenschaft* vol. 95, 1983, 229–237.

1990 "The Book of Job and the Task of Preaching," *Journal for Preachers*, Lent, 1990, 13–22.

1990 "Leadership: Exodus 32," *Quarterly Review*, Fall, 1990, vol. 10, no. 3, 46–68.

1991 Five articles for the *Anchor Bible Dictionary* (New York: Doubleday, 1992): "Zophar," "Eliphaz," "Jemimah," "Keren-Happuch," and "Keziah."

1993 "The Bible Becomes Literature: An Encounter with Ruth," *Word and World,* Spring, 1993, Vol. XIII, No. 2, 130–135.

1993 "Revelation According to Jacob and Mrs Turpin: Early Reflections on Preaching and Contemporary Literature," *Journal for Preachers,* Advent, 1993, 11–21.

1999 "What Does the Bible Say about Homosexuality?" in *Finishing the Journey,* Northaven United Methodist Church, 2000, 14–17. Reprinted in *American Journal of Pastoral Counseling,* Vol 3, Nos. 3/4, 2001, 153–155.

2003 "A Tight Squeeze," sermon published in *First Fruits,* eds. David Mosser and Brian Bauknight (Nashville: Abingdon Press, 2003), 73–82.

2008 Introduction and notes to "Job" (684–733) and "Ecclesiastes" (905–920) in *The Discipleship Study Bible,* eds. Bruce C. Birch, Brian K. Blount, Thomas G. Long, Gail R. O'Day, and W. Sibley Towner (Louisville: Westminster/John Knox Press, 2008).

2008 Entries "Job" (p. 81), "Laws and Regulations" (86–88), "Levitical Holiness Codes" (88–89), and "Pathos/Feeling" (358–360) in *The New Interpreter's Handbook of Preaching,* ed. Paul Scott Wilson (Nashville: Abingdon Press, 2008).

2009 "Preaching and the Creation," *Homiletic,* Vol. XXXIII, No.1, Summer, 2009, 1–11.

2009 Introduction and Commentary to the Book of Job (611–649) in *The Wesley Study Bible,* eds. Joel B. Green and William H. Willimon (Nashville: Abingdon Press, 2009).

2010 "Toward a Story Homiletic: History and Prospects," *Journal for Preachers,* Vol. XXXIII, No.3, pp.16–29.

2010 "Opening the Old Testament," Weekly Reflections on the Lectionary Text from the Old Testament, hosted by the website Patheos.com.

List of Contributors

Ronald J. Allen
  Professor of Preaching and Gospels and Letters
  Christian Theological Seminary

Walter Brueggemann
  William Marcellus McPheeters Professor Emeritus of Old Testament
  Columbia Theological Seminary

Roy L. Heller
  Associate Professor of Old Testament
  Perkins School of Theology, Southern Methodist University

Ruthanna B. Hooke
  Associate Professor of Homiletics
  Virginia Theological Seminary

Martha Myre
  A United Methodist elder and freelance writer who is developing a
    new ministry with college students.

Richard Nelson
  Associate Dean for Academic Affairs, W. J. A. Power Professor of
    Biblical Hebrew and Old Testament Interpretation
  Perkins School of Theology, Southern Methodist University

Richard Stern
  Professor of Homiletics
  Saint Meinrad Seminary and School of Theology

Steven Tuell
  James A. Kelso Associate Professor of Hebrew and Old Testament
  Pittsburgh Theological Seminary

Mary Donovan Turner
  Carl Patton Professor of Preaching, Dean of the Disciples Seminary
    Foundation
  Pacific School of Religion

Introduction

Whatever might have happened eschatologically to the early heretic Marcion, who rejected the Old Testament as Christian scripture, he must smile frequently at his intractable influence. In over 30 years of ministry in the church, I have encountered Marcion's ghost haunting many congregations. Far too many Christians consider the Old Testament as at best "background" material to the New Testament; far too many preachers ignore it when choosing sermon texts.

We co-edited this book as one effort to correct this "heresy" that shortchanges the spiritual life of the church. We drew inspiration for this project from the ministry of Dr. John C. Holbert, newly retired as the Lois Craddock Perkins Professor at Perkins School of Theology. Dr. Holbert dedicated his professional life to the advocacy of the value of the Old Testament for the church and its proclamation. He communicated to his students the adventure, poignancy, and complexity of the text. In his Exodus seminar the students could practically hear the furious clanging of the chariot wheels of the pursuing Egyptians as they imagined crossing the Sea of Reeds to escape. In a course on Job they experienced Job's revulsion at his own sufferings, hearing the potsherd scrape against his sores. They joined in his cowering reverence when, near the end of the book, God speaks to him out of the whirlwind. Through all of this, students realized both the difficulty of answering the why question of suffering and the necessity of continuing to struggle with that question (and the many other matters that Job treats).

The chapters of this book are written by gifted scholars, teachers, and preachers who share a love for the Old Testament. They write to honor Dr. Holbert and to insist on the urgency of the Old Testament for the pulpit. Each chapter takes up a provocative topic with regard to the Old Testament. The golden thread is that each topic connects the biblical text with the concerns of contemporary people.

For perhaps no other book has the church missed the point as for Jonah. Too many unrelenting and pointless arguments about the historicity of the great fish (a creative and brief literary device) detract from the abrupt but ultimately peacemaking message about God's love for one's most bitter enemy. Contributor Steven Tuell appreciates the literary character of the book, including its irony, satire, and comedy. He also juxtaposes Jonah with Nahum to initiate a theological dialogue.

Every pastor has heard the persistent assertion from lay folk that the Old Testament presents a wrathful, judgmental, punitive interpretation of God, while the New Testament proclaims a loving, forgiving God, incarnated in Jesus. Ronald J. Allen in his essay offers insightful corrective to this misunderstanding. By emphasizing the Old Testament message of God's *hesed* (loving kindness or faithful love) and desire for community well-being, Allen balances the divine role of Judge with the healing, atoning, and reconciling work of God in the Old Testament. Using prophetic and apocalyptic themes, Allen shows how the Old Testament examines suffering and pain, while revealing a God who seeks the well-being of all creation and every individual.

Everyone who stands in a pulpit or sits in a pew lives with regret. We all wince at mistakes, unable to undo them. The authors of the realistic narratives of the Bible knew this tendency well. They do not present flawless heroes, but patriarchs and matriarchs who made dreadful decisions and took contemptible actions. Yet God chose these bumblers and scoundrels to live out the divine plan. Martha Myre, scholar and pastor, helps preachers present these honest portrayals of biblical characters as God's instruments—people God used in spite of themselves.

A funny thing happened on the way to the completion of this volume. Dr. Mary Donovan Turner did not receive the emails from Dr. Alyce McKenzie giving instructions on Turner's chapter. An overzealous spam filter trapped those emails. The scrupulous spam filter did not want Dr. Turner's eyes to gaze upon emails about sexuality and eroticism in the Hebrew Bible. Contemporary society jumps the tracks in two different directions on the topic of sex. Like the uptight spam filter, we act squeamishly about sex. In the other direction, pornography and provocation lurk everywhere. Drawing on such texts as Hosea and Song of Songs, Dr. Turner addresses the role of the Old Testament in developing a healthy, joyous, non-exploitative understanding of sex.

Many voices decry the "extended adolescence" in society. What consequences follow from postponing adulthood and maturity? How does immaturity undermine progress for the community and for the church? Writing from a Lutheran perspective, Richard Nelson, established biblical scholar and colleague of John Holbert, shows preachers how to proclaim from Proverbs growth into maturity as gospel, or "good news." Drawing upon several texts from Proverbs, Nelson draws analogies to aspects of culture, even inner-city contexts.

Two types of books regularly occupy the best-seller lists: cookbooks and diet books. We feed our appetites and curse the results. We shell out for gym memberships and plastic surgery. How should the church understand our embodiment? Do we consider our bodies a curse or a blessing? What relationship exists between our physical needs and our spiritual needs? Using both narrative and poetic texts, Roy Heller unfolds the Hebrew understanding of the body and its senses, providing insight for a neglected but much-needed topic in preaching.

In exploring the role of movies in proclamation, Richard Stern ranges from the role of movies in contemporary narrative making to practical advice about using movie clips within an actual sermon. Movies have potential to bring a visual component to the sermon, but Stern offers wise counsel about the biases of Hollywood. He includes reflection on the "roundness" of Old Testament characters, suggesting that Christians today can identify with them more readily than with New Testament characters, who often appear only briefly. For the preacher caught in the demand for contact with culture and the commitment to integrity in treating the biblical witness, Stern offers sound guidance.

The Hebrew scriptures certainly demonstrate that a variety of types of literature can communicate the message of faith. The church tends to contrast the Bible with "secular" literature. Yet writers of poems, plays, and novels plumb the depth of human experience. Ruthanna Hooke, trained in theology and performance studies, identifies some common purposes for "worldly" literature and the literature in the Old Testament. She notes some tension between art and sermon, suggesting that art exists for its own sake, whereas the preacher embeds the sermon in liturgy. Nevertheless, the preacher has much to learn from the depth, creativity, and courage of the artist. Hooke offers suggestions about dialogue between specific poems and texts from Genesis and Psalms, as well as a sermon series on creation.

With characteristic creativity, well-known Old Testament scholar Walter Brueggemann draws on the bizarre, self-contained, and often ignored text of Elisha's bones giving life to a corpse (2 Kgs. 13:20–21). He employs these verses about the "radioactive" bones of the prophet to advocate for the continuing afterlife of prophetic texts, able to provide vitality after their original context has passed away. Prophetic oracles of judgment can revive a sense of shame that has flickered out. Oracles of promise inspire hope for concrete, historical possibilities, including Martin Luther King's "I Have a Dream" speech. Brueggemann fleshes out these possibilities with specific prophetic texts. All preachers desire for the sermon to generate life within the service and, long-term, within the congregation.

Our greatest hope is that this volume will play a part in the fulfillment of the promise of 2 Isaiah:

Just as the rain and the snow
Come down from the sky
And don't return there
Without watering the earth,

> Making it conceive and yield plants
> And providing seed to the sower
> And food to the eater,
> So is my word
> That comes from my mouth:
> It does not return to me empty.
> Instead, it does what I want,
> And accomplishes what I intend.
> (Isa. 55:10–11, CEB)

Charles L. Aaron, Ph.D.
Pastor, First United Methodist Church, Terrell, Texas

Alyce M. McKenzie, Ph.D.
Le Van Professor of Preaching and Worship, Perkins School of Theology, Dallas, Texas

1

You Can't Say That!
Preaching Jonah as a Comedy[1]

By Steven Tuell

Early in my teaching career, I met with a concerned parent who was deeply upset about what his son was learning in my Old Testament class. Specifically, this father was upset about the textbook we were using, Bernhard Word Anderson's classic *Understanding the Old Testament,* which at that time was the gold standard in Old Testament introductions for the college classroom. Even more specifically, he was upset about what Anderson had to say about Jonah:

> Many readers have recognized that the story is designed to tickle one's sense of humor. Surely the author did not have a straight face when telling how a big fish belched Jonah back in the direction from which he had come, that the Assyrian king immediately believed Jonah's preaching and commanded everyone–including livestock–to put on sackcloth, and that no sooner had Jonah settled down comfortably in the shade of the plant than Yahweh, the jokester, needled him further by sending a worm to eat the plant and a withering desert wind (sirocco) to boot.[2]

That Anderson went on to say, "The storyteller's humor and satire, however, only make the theological truth of the story more pointed,"[3] cut no ice with this gentleman at all. The very notion that a biblical text could be treated as comedy was, to him, blasphemous: You just can't say that about the Bible! Scripture, it seems, cannot be funny.

I have encountered similar problems with Jesus' use of humor and exaggeration.[4] Bible students often agonize over how to apply such obviously hyperbolic statements as "If your right eye causes you to sin, tear it out and throw it away" (Matt. 5:29).[5] Indeed, our reading of Jesus has been so relentlessly humorless that to explain his statement, "It is easier for a camel to go through the eye of a needle than for someone who is rich to enter the kingdom of God" (Mark 10:25; cf. Matt. 19:24; Luke 18:25), we have concocted an elaborate story about a tiny gate in the walls of Jerusalem through which a camel could pass only after being unloaded and getting down on its knees. Though this explanation is still found in some Bible handbooks, and though obliging Jerusalem tour guides will even show you the gate (an interesting trick, as the current wall was built by Suleiman the Magnificent between 1537 and 1541), a little reflection quickly reveals its unlikelihood: Why would you take a camel through such an awkward gate? Why, if there was such a gate, are the disciples so nonplussed by Jesus' statement as to ask, "Then who can be saved?" (Mark 10:26). No, Jesus asks us to imagine a literal camel passing through the eye of a literal needle. He is making a ridiculous, deliberately extreme, indeed humorous statement about the impossibility of salvation for the wealthy—or indeed, for anyone—outside of God's intervention (cf. Mark 10:27). That we do not get the joke says far more about the presuppositions that we bring to the text than it does about the text itself.

Jonah as a Comedy

Frederick Buechner has called the parables of Jesus "jokes about God," saying, "I believe that the comedy of them is not just a device for making the truth that they contain go down easy but that the truth that they contain can itself be thought of as comic."[6] Perhaps the same could be said of the book of Jonah. Certainly, Brevard Childs describes Jonah as "parable-like,"[7] and many interpreters would agree that Jonah is, broadly speaking, a comedy.[8] Indeed, only by reading Jonah as a comedy do we take seriously the book's most obvious feature: the persistent, deliberate exaggeration that makes this book *funny*.

Though the book of Jonah itself is small, everything in it is bigger than life. For example, a common element in prophetic call narratives is what Robert Gnuse calls "prophetic denial"—the objection of a prophet to her or his call, based on a sense of unworthiness or inability in the one called, or on anxiety about what the call implies.[9] Moses begs God to send someone else (Exod. 4:13); Jeremiah objects that he is too young (Jer. 1:6); Isaiah exclaims, "I am a man of unclean lips" (Isa. 6:5). But Jonah alone votes with his feet! Commanded by God, "Get up and go [Hebrew qum lek] to Nineveh" (Jon. 1:2, author's translation), Jonah instead "got up to flee" (Hebrew wayyaqom ... libroakh; author's translation) in the opposite direction toward Tarshish, "away from the presence of the LORD" (Jon. 1:3). The parallel structure here in the Hebrew, as well as the repeated phrase "from the presence of the LORD" (Hebrew millipne YHWH, found twice in Jon. 1:3 and again in 1:10), underlines Jonah's defiance. In all of Scripture, only Cain is also said to go out from God's presence (Gen. 4:16). We may object, of course, that God being God, Jonah cannot really flee from God's presence. But the first hearers of this story would surely have known this, too (cf. Ps. 139:7). As Millar Burrows observed, the audience of the book of Jonah, knowing full well that flight from God is impossible, would have understood the comic intent of this narrative from the beginning: "They would exchange knowing looks and settle down to enjoy what was coming, thinking, 'This is going to be good!'"[10]

Other examples of this book's larger-than-life character are readily identified. Scripture has no more extreme example of divine deliverance from death than Jonah, who is saved from drowning when he is swallowed by a giant fish (Jon. 1:17)–scarcely what we would normally call a rescue! The extravagant faith of the sailors, who in spite of Jonah's poor example become faithful worshippers of the Lord (1:16); the extravagant repentance of the Ninevites, who not only repent in sackcloth and ashes but cover their animals in sackcloth and ashes as well (3:7–9); the extravagant pique of Jonah, who in his bitterness at God's preservation of the city and his disappointment over the death of his shade plant is "angry enough to die" (4:9)–all are over the top, operatic in scale. Even the offhand statement that Nineveh "was an exceedingly large city, a three-day's walk across" (3:3) demonstrates Jonah's extravagance. Archaeological investigation reveals that until Nineveh became Assyria's capital city during the reign of Sennacherib (704–681 B.C.E.), it was a town about two miles in circumference. Thereafter, it quickly expanded to a city eight miles around, its outskirts spanning the Tigris: impressive, but still hardly a three-day's walk across.[11] An even more grandiose feature of Nineveh's description, however, is veiled by most English translations. Where the NRSV reads "an exceedingly large city," the Hebrew has 'ir-gedolah le'lohim: literally, "a large city of God"! While Koehler and Baumgartner note in their lexicon that the Hebrew 'elohim (usually rendered "God" or "gods") may be used as a superlative (a course that most English translations of Jon. 3:3 follow),[12] none of the examples for this usage that they list is uncontroverted.[13] Indeed, as Phyllis Trible notes, rendering the text with the English superlative, even if technically correct, falls short of the full implications in this verse: "Human calculations do not suffice; divine standards take the measure."[14]

The Purpose of Jonah

To preach Jonah faithfully, then, we must approach this book as a comedy.[15] But to what end is the comedy in Jonah directed? Some interpreters have understood Jonah to be a book of judgment and condemnation. Thomas Paine, perhaps the first to refer to Jonah explicitly as a satire, declared in his book *Age of Reason* (1807) that Jonah is "a book of the Gentiles," which "has been written as a fable, to expose the nonsense and satirize the vicious and malignant character of a Bible prophet."[16] Others have proposed that the prophet Jonah represents the attitudes of postexilic Judah, whose xenophobia this book satirically exposes. So, James Smart wrote, "In the years after the Exile there grew up in Israel a spirit of bitterness and vengefulness toward other lands"; in response, the book of Jonah seeks "to reawaken in the nation a sense of missionary destiny to which, as God's people, it had been called."[17] Indeed, a judgmental reading of Jonah is the inescapable consequence of reading this book as a satire. Literary critic Northrop Frye pithily described satire as "militant irony."[18] Since an attack presumes a target, the question for the reader of a satire inevitably becomes what, or who, is being satirized.[19] But apart from God's initial judgment on Nineveh, which Jonah is commissioned to announce (Jon. 1:1–2; 3:1–2), the theme of judgment simply is not present in this book. Even rebellious, recalcitrant Jonah gets a second chance (3:1). Indeed, in the book's final chapter, where Jonah confronts God with his accusation of faithlessness (God told Jonah to announce Nineveh's destruction, then didn't follow through), God reasons with the prophet rather than condemning him (4:9–11). Quite apart from the anti-Semitism implicit in some of these judgmental readings, they find no support in the book itself.

Another approach to the purpose of Jonah is to focus on repentance. R. E. Clements proposes, "[Jonah's] purpose is to assert the possibility of repentance, involving a complete change of heart on man's part, of which God will then take full account in his dealings with him."[20] The very success of the prophets, whose warnings regarding Israel and Judah had proven grimly accurate, had prompted a sense of fatalistic surrender; into this despair, Jonah's message brings hope: "Yet all men may repent, even the most hardened sinner and the most ungodly of men."[21] This seems a far more promising avenue for interpretation, and one far truer to the book's spirit, than the judgmental readings cited above. Further, reading Jonah as a book about repentance is in keeping with a strong stream of traditional Jewish interpretation. In the Mishnah (the compendium of rabbinic wisdom which, together with its commentary called the Gemara, makes up the Talmud), Nineveh is lifted up as an example of sincere repentance—an impression that the Babylonian Talmud (b. Taan. 16a) intensifies, urging faithful Israel to identify with the Ninevites in their repentance.[22] Indeed, Jonah is read in the synagogue on the afternoon of Yom Kippur: the day of fasting, self-examination, and repentance concluding the ten Days of Awe with which the Jewish year begins.[23] However, such a reading leaves the book's concluding act unexplained. Why, if the point of the book is repentance, are we left in the end with an unrepentant prophet?

The references to Jonah elsewhere in Scripture provide further evidence for the ways that this book was read by later communities of faith. In the Apocrypha, 5 Ezra 1:39 merely mentions Jonah as one of the Twelve Prophets, listed together with the Patriarchs Abraham, Isaac, and Jacob as the leaders of restored Israel.[24] In 3 Maccabees 6:8, however, the priest Eleazar mentions Jonah (with, intriguingly, no mention of the Ninevites), together with Daniel and his three companions, in his prayer for deliverance: "And Jonah, wasting away in the belly of a huge, sea-born monster, you, Father, watched over and restored unharmed to all his family." In the New Testament, Matthew refers twice to the "sign of Jonah" (Matt. 12:39–41 and 16:4) as the only sign of the in-breaking kingdom his "adulterous and sinful generation" would receive (the first of these references is paralleled in Luke 11:29–32; curiously, none of these passages is included in the Revised Common Lectionary). Jonah's three days in the fish's belly (Jon. 1:17 [Hebrew 2:1]) become a sign of Jesus' resurrection, paralleling his "three days and three nights…in the heart of the earth" (Matt. 12:40); as in 3 Maccabees, Jonah demonstrates God's gracious deliverance from death.[25] Further, as in the Mishnah and the Talmud, Nineveh is lifted up as an example of sincere repentance: "The people of Nineveh will rise up at the judgment with this generation and condemn it, because they repented at the proclamation of Jonah, and see, something greater than Jonah is here!" (Matt. 12:4 //Luke 11:32). Although Jonah is not mentioned, there are also clear parallels between Jonah 1 and the Gospel story of Jesus calming the storm (Matt. 8:18–27//Mark 4:35–41//Luke 8:22–25).[26] In each case, there is a "[great] storm."[27] Jesus, like Jonah, is asleep in the boat.[28] In each account, the sailors are delivered, and there is a calm after the storm.[29] Indeed, the many parallels between these accounts intensify the contrast between the faithful sailors in Jonah, who after their deliverance "feared the LORD exceedingly, and they offered a sacrifice to the LORD and made vows" (Jon. 1:16), and the faithless disciples in the Gospels, who ask, "Who then is this?" (Mark 4:41; cf. Matt. 18:27; Luke 8:25). In the Gospels, Jonah is remembered, not as a book about God's judgment, but as a book about God's deliverance.

God's Grace as the Theme of Jonah

Further insight into the purpose of the comedy in Jonah comes from Buechner's insightful reading of Jesus' parables as "jokes about God." The comic truth that the parables express, Buechner writes, is the same truth that made Sarah and Abraham laugh (Gen. 18:12–15) "until the tears rolled down their cheeks"–the "astonishing, gratuitous, hilarious…grace of God."[30] What makes the truth of God's grace comic is this very element of surprise and astonishment. As Buechner notes, "The tragic is inevitable. The comic is unforeseeable."[31] Northrop Frye similarly described comedies as sharing a distinctive shape, involving a surprising and fortuitous plot twist: "a series of misfortunes and misunderstandings brings the action to a threatening low point, after which some fortunate twist in the plot sends the conclusion up to a happy ending."[32] In this respect, Jonah does not, strictly speaking, follow the expected comic pattern. To be sure, God's gracious and miraculous provision of the fish qualifies as a "fortunate twist in the plot," resulting in Jonah's personal deliverance as well as in the deliverance of Nineveh. But while there is a happy ending for the Assyrian capital, Jonah's own story ends ambiguously, with the reader still wondering how Jonah will respond to God's final message of grace. Still, comedies can end without a neat resolution. Consider Woody Allen's *What's New, Pussycat?*, Mel Brooks' *Blazing Saddles*, or *Monty Python and the Holy Grail*, three film comedies that do not resolve but rather dissolve into chaos. Although Jonah is not nearly as anarchic as these modern examples of comedy, its disconcertingly open ending is a jarring note. As Abraham Heschel observes, "God's answer to Jonah, stressing the supremacy of compassion, upsets the possibility of looking for a rational coherence of God's ways with the world."[33]

God's surprising grace is the theme of the book of Jonah. This is demonstrated by the odd placement of Jonah 2:2–9 (Hebrew 3–10), a thanksgiving psalm celebrating God's deliverance of the psalmist from death:

> I went down to the land
> whose bars closed upon me forever;
> yet you brought up my life from the Pit,
> O LORD my God (Jon. 2:6 [7]).

While this psalm has clear parallels to poetry elsewhere in Scripture that deals with the descent into Sheol, the place of the dead, and its underworld ocean (e.g., 2 Sam. 22:17//Ps. 18:16; Ezek. 26:19–31; Pss. 42:7; 71:20; Song 8:6–7), it lacks such parallels to its immediate context. In particular, the psalmist speaks of the weeds wrapping about his head (2:5) as though he is sinking to the bottom alone, without any fishy vehicle to protect him. Since this psalm was almost certainly not composed for its current location,[34] its inclusion tells us something about the way Jonah's editors read this book. In the course of incorporating the book of Jonah into the canon, those reflecting on its meaning found this song of God's gracious deliverance an apt expression of Jonah's theology.[35] By this, of course, I mean the theology of the book, not of the prophet!

Jonah the prophet, within this narrative, clearly wants God to act according to divine justice rather than divine grace. Yet Jonah does express the theme of God's grace, however grudgingly. In explanation of his earlier flight from God's presence, the prophet declares: "'O LORD! Is not this what I said while I was still in my own country? That is why I fled to Tarshish at the beginning; for I knew that you are a gracious God and merciful, slow to anger, and abounding in steadfast love, and ready to relent from punishing'"

(Jon. 4:2). Jonah had not wanted to deliver the message of judgment against Nineveh he had been given because he knew that God was likely to "relent from punishing," leaving Jonah with the stamp of the false prophet, whose predictions do not come true (cf. Deut. 18:21–22)[36]–which is, of course, what happened. No wonder Jonah is angry! The prophet quotes here from the divine self-declaration in Exodus 34:6–7, a passage cited throughout Scripture, usually with a decided accent on God's grace and forgiveness (e.g., Pss. 86:15; 103:8; 145:8; Neh. 9:17; Joel 2:13). Intriguingly, this same passage is quoted with reference to Nineveh in Nahum 1:3. But Nahum and Jonah recall the Exodus text in different ways.[37] In Exodus, a statement of God's grace follows the statement of God's patience (Exod. 34:6: "slow to anger, *and abounding in steadfast love and faithfulness,*" emphasis mine). In Nahum, however, an assertion of God's might takes its place ("slow to anger *but great in power,*" Nah. 1:3; emphasis mine). Nahum not only alters the reference to God's grace in Exodus, but also (unlike the gracious citations of Exod. 34:6–7 listed above), quotes the line in Exodus 34:7 referring to punishment: "the LORD will by no means clear the guilty" (Hebrew wenaqqeh lo' yinaqqeh; cf. Num. 14:18; Jer. 30:11//46:28). Jonah does the opposite. Here, the prophet not only recalls God's "steadfast love," but also describes God as "ready to relent from punishing" (Hebrew wenikham 'al-hara'ah)! It is likely that the writer of Jonah has chosen to use wenikham ("relent") here to pun with wenaqqeh ("declare innocent; clear") in Exodus and in Nahum, underlining and reemphasizing God's gracious choice to preserve Nineveh.

Jonah and Nahum: Insights from a Canonical Reading

The depictions of Nineveh in Nahum and in Jonah stand curiously at odds. In Nahum, Nineveh is thoroughly evil and destined for a well-deserved destruction (cf. Nah. 3:1–7). But in Jonah, Nineveh becomes an example of earnest, extravagant repentance, to which God graciously responds with salvation (Jon. 3:5–9). One solution to this tension comes from the relative dating of these two books. The oracles of Nahum (Nah. 2–3) were written in the mid to late seventh century B.C.E.,[38] in the white heat of hatred for an oppressor whose atrocities were still fresh. Jonah was written much later, in the period after the exile,[39] at a sufficient remove that it was possible to use Israel's ancient enemy as a demonstration of God's grace.

However, Jonah and Nahum are not merely separate books, with their own divergent histories. They are also two parts of a larger collection of twelve short prophetic books, commonly called the Minor Prophets but more properly understood, in keeping with ancient Jewish and Christian tradition, as the Book of the Twelve. Increasingly, recent scholarship has taken the designation of the Twelve as a book seriously, pushing the interpreter of Jonah to think about its placement within the Book of the Twelve, and its relationship with others among the Twelve.[40] In our Old

Testament, Jonah is found before Micah, which sets the book literarily in the mid-eighth century setting of "Jonah son of Amittai, the prophet" (2 Kgs. 14:25), who prophesied in the days of Jeroboam II (788–747 B.C.E.). So, while Jonah was written after Nahum, the canonical structure of the Book of the Twelve invites us to read Jonah before Nahum.[41] The narrative logic of the Twelve compels us to ask what went wrong: How did Nineveh go so far astray? Targum Jonathan (a translation of the prophets into Aramaic for use in the synagogue) addresses this question in the first verse of Nahum:

> The oracle of the cup of the curse Nineveh was to drink. In former times, Jonah son of Amittai, the prophet from Gath Hepher, prophesied against her, and she repented from her sins, but then, when she sinned again [Aramaic *de'osephath lemikhye*], Nahum of the house of Qoshi prophesied against her again [Aramaic *tab*; the same root is used to describe Nineveh's repentance (*wetabath*)], as is written in this book (Nah. 1:1, my translation).

Similarly, the early Christian commentator Theodoret of Cyrus (fifth century C.E.), noting the patience of God described in Nahum 1:3, says "You Ninevites are witnesses to this, practicing repentance and finding salvation, and then guilty of extreme wickedness and for a time not paying the penalty for it."[42] One solution to this puzzle, then, is that Nineveh, after having repented, fell once more into sinfulness. Another would be to question whether Nineveh ever really repented in the first place. Unlike the Mishnah and the Babylonian Talmud, the Jerusalem Talmud questions Nineveh's sincerity (y. Taan. 65b).[43] Similarly, in his lectures on Jonah, John Calvin states, "I know not whether that was a true and legitimate conversion… but it seems more probable, that they were induced by the reproofs and threatening of the Prophet, suppliantly to deprecate the impending wrath of God: hence God once forgave them….there is certainly no reason to think that they had really and from the heart repented."[44]

By either reading, though, the Book of the Twelve urges its readers not to take God's forgiveness for granted. Although the Lord is "a gracious God and merciful, slow to anger, and abounding in steadfast love, and ready to relent from punishing" (Jon. 4:2; cf. Exod. 34:6–7 and Nah. 1:3), it is disastrous to presume upon the Lord's grace. Reading canonically, Nahum reminds the reader that the grace of God celebrated in Jonah is not cheap–a truth that Christian readers, living on the far side of the cross, should know all too well (cf. the warnings against presumption in Heb. 6:4–6; 10:26–27; 1 John. 3:6–9). Jonah, in turn, provides a gracious contrast to Nahum's violent rejection of the foreigner; as Jim Nogalski observes, Jonah "*presumes* the nations can have a salvific relationship with the God of Israel [emphasis his]."[45] If we are to do justice to Jonah homiletically then, we must begin on a sound exegetical base by recognizing that this book is about the comic surprise of God's extravagant grace.

Preaching Jonah

The lectionary preacher will find only two opportunities to preach from Jonah in the three-year cycle of the Revised Common Lectionary. In Year B, Jonah 3:1–5, 10 is the Old Testament reading for the Third Sunday after Epiphany.[46] The Gospel for that Sunday is Mark 1:14–20, the beginning of Jesus' ministry, a pairing that suggests a missionary approach to Jonah.[47] Although this reading does have some merit (Jonah is, after all, sent to a foreign field, and he does succeed in winning some converts on the boat), be careful to recall that it is God's grace that is the book's primary theme (as this passage from Jonah emphasizes; cf. Jonah 3:10). By selectively focusing on the "success" of Jonah's mission to Nineveh, this lection could prompt a sermon promising the success of our own outreach and mission, which would miss the point. Do not leave unaddressed the prophet's comically extravagant reluctance. Although Nineveh is a three-day's journey across, Jonah goes in only a day's journey—just far enough in to say that he has been to Nineveh and has the T-shirt. He stays only long enough to deliver his pronouncement of doom, and then he leaves. But astonishingly, the Ninevites repent anyway, and God responds with forgiveness. Nineveh is spared, not so much because of, but nearly in spite of, Jonah's mission! Jonah does not "save" Nineveh; still less can we "save" either the people in some foreign field or the unchurched in our own neighborhoods. Only God can save. In the Gospel for this day, Jesus announces not his own reign but God's (Mark 1:15); we too do well to remember that the kingdom of God is God's kingdom, not ours. God acts in our world and invites us to participate in God's activity—a message particularly appropriate to the season after Epiphany, which celebrates God's gracious self-revelation.

The other opportunity to preach Jonah in the lectionary comes in Year A, Proper 20, in the season after Pentecost. For this Sunday, Jonah 3:10–4:11 is given as an alternate[48] to the Old Testament reading for the day (Exod. 16:2–15, God's provision of mannah), to go with the Gospel[49] (Matt. 20:1–17, the parable of the laborers in the vineyard). In this famously difficult parable, a landowner chooses to pay all his day laborers the same wage, whether they had worked all day or had just joined the crew in the final hour; the parable ends with the landowner's question, "Or are you envious because I am generous?" (Matt.1:16), followed by Jesus' declaration, "So the last shall be first and the first shall be last." One reading of this parable supports the judgmental interpretations of Jonah rejected above, embracing the Gentiles who have come late to the Lord, and castigating the Jews for their Jonah-esque narrowness and lack of generosity. Indeed, the boundaries of the Old Testament lection, giving the bulk of the space to Jonah's resentment, may fuel this reading. But the book of Jonah gives the last word to God, not to the prophet. The NRSV renders the verb *khus* in Jonah 4:11 as "be concerned about," which captures the parallel between God's concern about Nineveh and Jonah's concern for his shade plant, expressed by the same verb (Jon. 4:10). However, the word would better be rendered as "have compassion for" (cf. Joel 2:17; Ps. 72:13).[50] As Abraham Heschel wrote regarding this verse, "beyond justice and anger lies the mystery of compassion."[51] The theme of Jonah is not judgment, after all, but God's extravagant grace. Rather than the parable prompting a judgmental reading of the first lection, the influence can–and should–work in the opposite direction. Jonah focuses our reading of the Gospel, not on the understandable resentment of those who had worked all day, but on the unexpected generosity of the landowner to those who had been looking for work all day. By hiring those desperate people even at that late hour and then paying them a full day's wage, this landowner has, like the Lord in Jonah, chosen compassion over justice. In these days of widespread unemployment and unprecedented income inequality, that message strikes a powerful chord.

The preacher who wishes to explore more fully the implications of Jonah as a comic parable of God's grace–or, to adapt Buechner's phrase, as "a joke about God"– would do better to abandon the common lectionary for a time and follow the strategy of *lectio continua,* preaching straight through the book. An excellent time for such a series would be the season after Epiphany, which is devoted to exploring the implications of God's gracious revelation in Christ. Each of Jonah's four chapters is a coherent unit, so an exegetically responsible procedure would be to explore the text in a series of four sermons, each examining an aspect of God's grace. Be sure, in each sermon, to express the hilarious extravagance of God's grace, lavished upon us. So, in Jonah 1, God's grace is both reflected in the kindness of the sailors toward Jonah (1:13), and also experienced by the sailors in their deliverance from the storm, resulting in their becoming followers of the Lord (1:16)–something that the Ninevites do not do. Particularly in the first Sunday after Epiphany, a parallel may be drawn between these foreign sailors and the foreign wise men in Matthew 2:1–12. In the psalm of deliverance in Jonah 2, particularly with its prose introduction (1:17–2:1 [2:1–2 in the Hebrew])[52] and conclusion (2:10 [11]) concerning the great fish, Jonah himself experiences God's grace in the midst of trouble. A fitting Gospel parallel to this passage would be Matthew 12:39–41 or Luke 11:29–32, dealing with the sign of Jonah–Gospel passages that do not have a home in the Revised Common Lectionary. In Jonah 3, God's grace is manifest in God's responsiveness to the repentance of Nineveh, so that the city is spared. You may consider pairing this chapter with one of Paul's powerful justification texts, such as Romans 5:1–11. Finally, Jonah 4 raises questions about God's grace that may be familiar to us: Is it really fair for grace to be shown to the undeserving? What role do we play on our own salvation, apart from being its grateful recipients? A worthwhile conversation partner for this Old Testament reading may be James 2:14–16, which reminds us that a living faith and a transformed life belong together. To move in another direction with Jonah 4, consider reading this passage against Galatians 2:15–21, with its radical emphasis on God's grace alone.

Another way to do a series exploring God's grace in Jonah would be to follow John Wesley's description of the action of grace in three parts, as prevenient, justifying, and sanctifying grace.[53] Jonah 1 could then point toward God's prevenient grace, active before we are aware of it and enabling us to respond to Christ. Prevenient grace may be seen operating in the sailors, preparing them to respond to the Lord, even though God's messenger is sadly wanting! An intriguing contrast would be to read this text over against one of the Gospel stories of the calming of the storm (Matt. 8:18–27//Mark 4:35–41//Luke 8:22–25). Jonah 3, with its depiction of the repentance of the Ninevites and of God's response to them, is as we have seen a perfect demonstration of justifying grace. The final chapter, then, would point toward sanctifying grace–particularly given its open-endedness. How will Jonah respond to God's offer to see life through the lens of God's love and grace? The book invites us to place ourselves in Jonah's shoes, and so to ask this question of ourselves as well. A fitting New Testament parallel text would be Philippians 4:4–9, the practical admonitions to Christian living toward the end of what may be Paul's most loving and gracious epistle. Should you follow this preaching strategy, the psalm in Jonah 2 could be used in all three Sundays as a responsive reading, or you could mine its phrases for calls to worship and corporate prayers.

Reading and preaching Jonah as a comedy may prepare us, and our congregations, to see the comic surprise of God's grace elsewhere, in life and in Scripture. But some, in well-meaning piety, will shrink from such frivolity, thinking that faith ought to be serious business. When you say that Jonah (let alone Jesus) is funny, they may well respond, "You can't say that!" As I write this, snow is falling outside my window, and Christmas is just around the corner. I find myself thinking of the humorless Protestant Roundheads in Cromwell's England, who tried to stamp out the unseemly celebration of Yuletide. Sadly, as the annual rants about the supposed "war on Christmas" once more ring out over the airwaves,[54] and as various voices once more pick up the urgent call for us to "Keep Christ in Christmas" (as though anyone could keep him out!), it is clear that that prim, humorless spirit is still abroad in the church. Yet Northrop Frye described the Bible itself, in its entirety, as a comedy, in which humanity "loses the tree and water of life at the beginning of Genesis and gets them back at the end of Revelation."[55] The "fortunate twist in the plot" of Scripture is the cross of Jesus Christ, the nadir up from which history, however shakily and uncertainly, now rises toward its culmination with Christ's return at the end of the age (cf. Phil. 2:6–11). That the Bible is a comedy says something profoundly significant about God and about life in the world. Many modern philosophers have viewed life as a tragedy into which we are hurled without direction or guidance. But the Christian confession is that life is a comedy: a celebration of joy and possibility. We can make this confession, over against the often tragic events of life, because we get the joke. The extravagant, hilarious grace of God gives us hope for the future.

2

Being Sent to the Principal's Office: Who God Is Not in the Old Testament

By Ronald J. Allen

Through twelve years of public school, I was sent to the principal's office only once. I sat outside the office, stomach tight, chest pounding, and my heart sinking. I had never actually spoken with our principal, but I had seen those bullet-like eyes freeze a student who had cut into the lunch line ahead of where that student should have been, and I had heard that chainsaw voice cut down students wrestling in the hallway. As I sat in the stiff wooden chair next to her office, I wondered if my life, as I had known it, was about to end.

Many people imagine God as such a principal: hard, unbending, gruff, and punitive. They think of God as a judge who monitors their lives, and they worry that God will condemn them and their loved ones. At the other end of the interpretive spectrum, some people do not believe God punishes individuals or communities because a God of love would never do something hurtful. Some Christians contrast the stern God of the Torah, Prophets, and Writings with the loving God of the Gospels and Letters.[1] This chapter wrestles with the notion of God as harsh principal in light of the deepest convictions about God in the Torah, Prophets, and Writings.

The Deepest Convictions about God in the Torah, Prophets, and Writings

The Torah, Prophets, and Writings are a diverse body of material containing different kinds of literature and different worldviews and theologies. Thus to attempt to name the deepest convictions about God in the Hebrew Bible is to risk oversimplification. Nevertheless, many scholars believe that the Bible gives us fundamental clues as to the character and actions of the One who sits in the principal's office of the universe.

We may identify key convictions concerning God in the Torah, Prophets, and Writings. While I discuss these qualities individually, they actually intertwine. Furthermore, the different theological families in the Torah, Prophets, and Writings view these convictions differently, especially the priestly, deuteronomic, and apocalyptic theologies,[2] but also wisdom theologies. God seeks to promote the inclusive well-being of individuals, Israel, the Gentiles, and the natural world.[3]

God Created the World for Inclusive Well-Being

The Hebrew Bible assumes that God created the world and continues to sustain it. The priestly theologians begin the Bible with the theopoetic description of creation in Genesis 1:1–2:4a. Before God began to give the world its present form, the earth was a wild primeval sea; the existing elements were a chaos in which they had energy, but the energy was unfocused and even destructive. Indeed, Israelite writers often used the sea as a symbol of chaos.

In the act of creation, God brings order out of chaos. The ordering is to create a universe in which all things are good (*tov*). In this context, to be "good" means to manifest the qualities necessary to fulfill God's purposes. God's purpose is for all elements of creation—land, water, skies, vegetation, fish, animals, birds, and human beings—to live together in mutually supportive relationships so that all things experience inclusive well-being. The special role of human beings is to exercise dominion. That is, in their small spheres, human beings are to do what God does in the cosmic sphere: help all elements of creation relate with one another so that all experience inclusive well-being. God is the principal of the universe, and human beings are vice principals with responsibilities similar to God's but with much smaller jurisdictions.

Whereas God created by the word in Genesis 1, sages picture God creating by means of wisdom, God's feminine agent. According to Proverbs 8:22–31, wisdom carries out the nuts-and-bolts work of creation. God fills the world with wisdom so that human beings can discover wisdom through experience. Proverbs 8:32–36 states the goal of finding wisdom: to be happy, that is, to live in the way that fulfills God's purposes for life (cf. Prov. 3:13–18).

Although only a handful of passages in the Torah, Prophets, and Writings are fully apocalyptic, these writings make a germane point: God's goal is to re-create the universe as a realm in which all things fully and forever take place according to God's design.[4] Zechariah, for example, anticipates the time when "Living waters shall flow out from Jerusalem, half of them to the eastern sea and half of them to the western sea; it shall continue in summer as in winter. And [God] shall become [ruler] over all the earth...and Jerusalem shall abide in security" (Zech. 14:8–11, passim). To be sure, this transformation includes God punishing those who violate the divine ways (a theme we discuss below).

God Is Faithful

One of the most pervasive and fundamental affirmations about God in the Torah, Prophets, and Writings is that God is faithful. An important biblical word to describe God's faithfulness is the Hebrew *hesed.*[5] This complex idea cannot be translated by a single English word. Katherine Doob Sakenfeld, who teaches at Princeton Theological Seminary, notes that *hesed* is often rendered by interconnected words and phrases such as steadfast love, loving kindness, loyalty, covenantal solidarity, grace, mercy, and goodness.[6]

The following are among the themes associated with *hesed.* It expresses God's unwavering commitment to community; it bespeaks God providing for the needs of the community, especially when the community is imperiled and/or in need of forgiveness; it derives from a God who is free and who cannot be coerced.[7] Divine *hesed* is the conviction that God is utterly trustworthy. "Thus divine loyalty (*hesed*) may be viewed generally as the very basis of Israel's life."[8]

We can see the centrality of *hesed* in relationship to other important qualities of God in Exodus 34:6. In the wake of the community's apostasy at Mt. Sinai, the priestly theologian describes God as "merciful and gracious, slow to anger, and abounding in steadfast love [*rav hesed*] and faithfulness, keeping steadfast love for the thousandth generation, forgiving iniquity and transgression and sin, yet by no means clearing the guilty" (cf. Isa. 54:8, 10). Psalm 136 speaks for many passages in regarding God's steadfast love (*hesed*) as the reason for the creation of the world, giving food to all flesh, and, by implication, sustaining the entire world as well as preserving Israel in the face of threat (Ps. 136; note vv. 4–9, 25).

God Makes and Keeps Covenant

A covenant is a promise of commitment from one party to another and is sometimes reciprocal. The Bible refers to God making several covenants. Most covenants in the Bible manifest the characteristics of a reciprocal covenant, common in the Ancient Near East, between more powerful and less powerful parties. Covenants presume that God makes promises to human beings and sets out instructions by which human beings are to live in order to enjoy the full blessing of the covenant. A covenant often notes negative consequences if the community fails to live according to the guidelines in the covenant. Human beings accept the covenant and agree to live according to its guidelines or face the consequences. God's purpose in covenant is to guide communities in the ways of inclusive well-being. A covenant spells out what people can count on from God, and what they should be able to count on from one another.[9]

Using language reminiscent of the deuteronomists, we summarize covenantal thinking as follows: God promises to bless those with whom God makes covenant. God sets out guidelines by which people can live with one another and with nature to receive fullness of blessing. When the community is obedient, God blesses the community. When the community is disobedient, God curses the community. However, the curse is not an end. The curse is intended to awaken the community to the fact that it is not blessed and, consequently, has the opportunity to repent—to turn away from disobedience and to become obedient and, hence, be blessed.

The biblical covenants are acts of grace. They originate in God's unmerited favor, and they embody divine *hesed.* Obedience does not earn blessing but instead is a positive response to the unmerited favor. Obedience is the community's "Yes!" to the covenant. A person or group does not follow the law to earn God's love but to express that love.

A review of the six main covenantal streams in the Torah, Prophets, and Writings reinforces the notion that God's foundational purpose in making covenant is well-being.

- The priestly theologians presuppose that God created the elements of the world to work together for inclusive well-being (Gen. 1:1–2:25) and that God continues to be actively involved in the world. Though the covenantal nature of creation is not directly stated, it is implied.
- The priestly theologians formalize God's covenant with the world as a whole. The flood demonstrated the consequences of disobedience. However, in Genesis 8:22, God covenants to preserve creation so that all people could be blessed. In Genesis 9:1–17, God spells out the terms of this covenant, prohibiting murder and teaching the violent that they can expect violence to be visited upon them.[10]
- According to the priestly theologians, God makes covenant with Sarai, Abram, and their descendants, not only to bless them, but so the life of Israel could model the way to blessing for all other human families (Gen. 12:1–3).
- According to Exodus (reflecting priestly influence), God instructs Israel at Sinai on how to live as a covenantal community by

enumerating the laws to direct their life in the way of blessing (e.g. Ex. 19:1–23;33; 24:1–8; 34:10–28; Lev. 26:3–46).

- The deuteronomic theologians also interpret covenant as the way to blessing. The deuteronomists name specific blessings and curses that follow from obedience and disobedience (Deut. 27 and 28). The deuteronomic perspective is in the background of Joshua, Judges, the Samuels, and the Kings. While the deuteronomists demarcate an everlasting covenant with David (2 Sam. 7), the books of Samuel and Kings tell the story of the sins and downfall of the monarchy to impress upon the reader the idea that the community (and its leaders) must live according to Torah or suffer curse (as Israel did by going into exile).

- Apocalyptic theology projects these themes onto a cosmic scale. The fall (Gen. 3:1–13) caused God to curse human beings and nature (Gen. 3:14–19). When the flood failed to prompt lasting repentance, God chose Sarai and Abram and their descendants to model the way to blessing. Yet, many individual Israelites and Israel as community suffered unjustly in the old age. To keep the divine promise to bless Israel and to bless all–and to prove God's faithfulness–God resolved to end the old age in a massive apocalypse and bring about a new era of history, the final and complete Realm of God. The faithful would then enjoy inclusive well-being forever (while the unfaithful suffered in hell).

While the motif of covenant is not central to the wisdom literature, the sages think that God is actively committed to the world and that God graciously fills the world with the knowledge that leads to blessing (e.g. Prov. 2:1–22). Those who "walk in the way of the good and keep to the paths of the just" will "abide in the land" in prosperity while "the wicked will be cut off."

When the Bible Pictures God as a Harsh Principal

We have found in our review thus far that God's overarching purpose is to bring about inclusive well-being. God is not fundamentally punishing or wrathful. Nevertheless, the Torah, Prophets, and Writings picture God causing or permitting evil in three cases.

First, God actively curses individuals and communities who violate God's purposes, particularly Israel.[11] This chastening sometimes takes place over generations so that people not originally involved in violation pay a price. Nevertheless, the goal of punishment was to call the community to repent and to live faithfully so that they could experience inclusive blessing.[12]

The priestly and deuteronomic theologians did not think God intended for judgment to be an end but to be remedial. They thought of God as similar to a parent who punishes a child, hoping the punishment would motivate better behavior.

The motif of punishment in response to disobedience intensifies in the apocalyptic writings that depict God consigning the wicked to hell. For instance, the book of Enoch, written about the second century B.C.E., develops an idea that becomes important in the Gospels and Letters. Enoch believed that the present age of history would climax with a great day of judgment. He received a vision as if he were an eyewitness to the final judgment:

> Behold, I saw all of them [a group of unfaithful leaders] bound, and they all stood before [God]. The [God's] judgment took place. First among the stars, they received their judgment and were found guilty, and they went to the place of condemnation; and they were thrown into an abyss, full of fire and flame, and full of the pillar of fire (1 Enoch 90:23–24).[13]

While occasional apocalyptic writers depict such punishment as a temporary refiner's fire in which the goal is to purify evildoers for life in the new world (the Realm of God), most apocalyptic theologians regard such punishment as everlasting.

While Christians sometimes claim that the God of the Torah, Prophets, and Writings is wrathful whereas the God of Jesus and the Gospels and Letters is loving, we must recognize that the idea of hell as a place of eternal (or remedial) torment does not appear extensively in the Torah, Prophets, and Writings. The idea of hell became fully developed in Jewish apocalyptic writings after most of the Torah, Prophets, and Writings were completed. The idea of God consigning people to hell appears much more strongly in the Gospels and Letters. For instance, at the end of the parable of the great judgment, the Matthean Jesus avers, "Truly, I tell you, just as you did not do it to one of the least of these, you did not do it to me. And these will go away into eternal punishment, but the righteous into eternal life" (Matt. 25:45–46).

First, the purpose of the apocalyptic teaching was to motivate the community to remain faithful. The suffering of the present age tempted the congregation to desert God and make an alliance with the evil powers of the present, but the apocalyptic writer reminded the community that unimaginable suffering awaited the unfaithful. Such passages also served as pastoral warnings for those outside the community: Outsiders who violated God's purposes could expect similar punishment. Hence, apocalyptic teaching implicitly invited evildoers to repent.

Second, some biblical writers depict God sending violence upon non-Israelite peoples who stand in the way of His purposes but who had little knowledge of those purposes. For instance, according to the deuteronomists, when Israel entered the Promised Land, Joshua ordered the Israelites to kill all of the inhabitants, including sheep and donkeys (Josh. 6:17, 21). Contemporary readers should see in these passages at attempt by the biblical writers to assure Israel that God had the will and power to keep the divine promises.

Third, God permits the innocent to suffer for no apparent reason. The book of Job pictures God permitting Job to suffer in this way.[14] Job was faithful and prosperous. However, a member of the divine court (Satan) makes a bet with God that Satan can cause Job to suffer so much that Job will curse God. The book of Job thus depicts God allowing the innocent Job to suffer. To be sure, the main purpose of the book of Job is to protest the simple deuteronomic formula that obedience produces blessing, and disobedience brings about suffering. Nevertheless, the book of Job makes no protest against Job's innocent suffering.

Theological Problems with the Harsh Principal, and a Resolution

Many preachers and congregants assume the theological validity of some or all of the three pictures of God as harsh principal just discussed. Some Christians believe that God unilaterally punishes those who stand in the way of God's purposes. Such punishment may take place directly; for instance, God may make a person sick. Or the punishment may take place through people or events in history as when God causes or allows a nation to fall. Few Christians in this category believe that every sickness, natural disaster, or other evil is the direct result of sin.

Nevertheless, Christians put forward multiple reasons for such occurrences. Even when believing that God does not actively *send* suffering, many Christians believe that God *permits* such things. God could intervene and prevent pain but does not do so. Christians sometimes struggle theologically with why God causes or allows such things, often concluding that God has some purpose for such suffering, even if we cannot confidently articulate that purpose. In the broad sense, then, God is responsible (even through passive permission giving) for such seasons of difficulty in the lives of individuals, communities, and nature.

However, I join a number of preachers and congregations in believing that God does not actively or passively authorize suffering. The deepest convictions concerning God in the Torah, Prophets, and Writings point in this direction. The idea that God would directly bring about pain goes against the idea that God's fundamental intention for created life is inclusive well-being. From this point of view, it is a contradiction to think that the God of *hesed* would cause or permit suffering. Where is inclusive well-being in Joshua ordering the deaths of the Canaanites or in God agreeing to allow Job to suffer in order to decide a bet?

Responsible Christian theology would agree that God does not cause the suffering of the innocent (such as Job), but many would assert that

God curses those who get in the way of His purposes. The covenants with creation and with Noah presuppose that everyone can know something of God's purposes. The book of Romans is explicit in this regard (Rom. 1:19–20). Many Christians further believe that God causes suffering to those who are familiar with the covenant because the covenant itself explains that disobedience begets curse.

However, in my view, the idea that God would cause pain, even when intended to spur repentance, contradicts the conviction of God's *hesed* seeking well-being for all. Pain is pain, and it disrupts well-being even when it is designed to promote repentance. Suffering is suffering, even when intended to bring about a change of heart. The God of *hesed* cannot order people to gun down other people. From my point of view as a process theologian, God is present in every situation to offer participants as much well-being as possible within the possibilities and limits of the situation. God always seeks the best for all, but God does not have the singular power to shape or reshape a situation. God works through cooperation with human beings and even with nature.

The easiest situations to explain from my perspective involve human choice. Human beings may choose to ignore God's invitation to well-being. In that case, *we invite negative consequences upon ourselves.* God does not directly authorize punishment, but we bring curse on ourselves. When we become cognizant of our derelict conditions, we have the opportunity to repent and to align ourselves with God's purposes.

Yet, all pain does not result from human decisions. Some forms of suffering do not come about because of poor human choices. Many illnesses, for example, simply befall people. Many disasters in nature appear to have no human root.

When our choices leave individuals and communities broken, and when circumstances leave people and nature in disarray, God is present with a lure toward the highest qualities of well-being possible in those situations. This perspective is consistent with the ideas of God acting for inclusive well-being and in *hesed*. A key element of God's covenant with humankind and nature is never to stop working for the good of all.

The Torah, Prophets, Writings, Gospels, and Letters never fully articulate my viewpoint. However, as indicated in the preceding paragraphs, I believe my view is consistent with the deepest convictions about God in that literature.

Three Passages Pointing to a God of *Hesed,* Covenant, and Inclusive Well-Being

We now bring these ideas to bear on three passages from Year C in the Revised Common Lectionary: Isaiah 55:1–9; Isaiah 66:10–14; Hosea 11:1–11. The preacher's conversation with the texts needs to recover enduring elements and to critique other aspects.

Isaiah 55:1–9 (Proper 9, Third Sunday in Lent)

The book of Isaiah divides into three parts. God made covenant with Judah. However, chapters 1–39 (often called First Isaiah) chronicle an era in which many in Israel abandoned the covenant by worshipping idols, exploiting the poor, and engaging in injustice (e.g. Isa. 1:2–20; 5:8–24). As a result, the curse fell upon Judah when God used the Babylonians to defeat Judah and send many of its leaders into exile (597–539 B.C.E.). A second prophet, Second Isaiah or Deutero-Isaiah, spoke chapters 40–55 during the exile. By the time of Second Isaiah, the prophet believed that Judah had been punished enough. The prophet invites the exiles to return to obedience so God would return them to the land of Judah. Third Isaiah (Isa. 56–66) prophesied after the people returned to Jerusalem. Isaiah 55:1–9 is the climax of Second Isaiah's message.

Today's text divides into three parts, each illustrating leading themes of Second Isaiah.

1. Many scholars think that the language of 55:1–2 is drawn from the practice of Ancient Near Eastern monarchs serving a banquet to celebrate the beginning of their reigns. These verses assume that God is preparing for such an occasion. In ancient practice, the host sent messengers in the manner of verses 1–2 to invite people to the meal. This part of the passage assures the community that God is acting to return them home and urges them to accept God's invitation.

2. Verses 3–5 reveal that God is transforming the community's identity and mission. Isaiah reaffirms the covenant with David (v. 3). However, Isaiah shifts the locus from David and his family to the community as a whole (v. 4). The people will now share in the ministry of David (v. 4). Scholars sometimes refer to this phenomenon as democratizing. From the standpoint of Isaiah (a priestly theologian), the purpose of this ministry is to model God's ways for other nations–gentiles–who will then come to the God of Israel in order to be blessed (v. 5).

3. In the final section, verses 5–9, Isaiah implores the community to accept God's invitation. Verse 5 confirms that God is present. Verse 6 calls the congregation to repent of the sins that got the community into exile. Verses 8–9 are not a general abstraction about God's ways being mysterious, but rather make a specific and contextual assertion: Yes, God is fulfilling the promises to David and the community by restoring the life of Judah, but the purpose of the community is to witness to the nations, the gentiles. Judahites may have assumed that God was regenerating their own blessing, but the prophet wants them to see that God has a higher plan.

The preacher might explore similarities between the situation of Judah in exile and that of today's congregation. How does the congregation feel as though they are in exile? Where does the preacher see signs that God is at work to restore the community? The sermon could alert the congregation to such developments and invite them to join God in the restoration.

In the spirit of Isaiah, the preacher could emphasize that God restores today's church so that it can witness to those who do not experience inclusive well-being. The assurance of this text is simultaneously a call to mission. The preacher can help the congregation identify the people and circumstances with whom it can enter into solidarity.

If the text falls on a Sunday when the congregation partakes of the loaf and the cup, the preacher could interpret the sacred meal as celebratory banquet of the kind assumed in Isaiah 55:1–2. To be sure, pain, exploitation, and violence continue. But the bread and the cup assure the congregation that we are never alone in such circumstances. The God of *hesed* is present.

Isaiah 66:10–14 (Proper 9)

Third Isaiah preached in Judah after the exiles returned from Babylon. Second Isaiah had predicted the return would be a second exodus concluding in a joyous homecoming (e.g. Isa. 43:1–7). Instead, the returnees found a land in chaos. The temple was in ruins; efforts to rebuild languished. The economy was depressed. Fields were destroyed. Conflict developed between those who stayed behind and those who had been in Babylon. Judah was not an independent state but was a colony of Persia. Many Judahites experienced the return as a disappointment. Third Isaiah assures the community that the covenant-keeping God will be faithful to the promises made through Second Isaiah. God will restore the community.

Third Isaiah marks a transition in theology in Israel. This prophet signals a much more pronounced movement toward apocalypticism. In its complete form, apocalypticism holds that God will intervene in history in a singular dramatic moment, destroying evil and recreating the world to reflect inclusive well-being. Isaiah 66 is not fully developed apocalyptic theology, but it contains impulses toward apocalyptic motifs.[15] The literary setting for today's passage begins in Isaiah 66:7–9. The prophet compares the situation in Judah with that of a pregnant woman. A pregnancy is long, and the pain of labor accompanies the act of giving birth. The rebuilding of the community will similarly take a long time and will involve struggle. Yet, just as a woman in labor eventually gives birth, so the congregation can count on restoration, albeit preceded by struggle. An apocalyptic prescience emerges in v. 8: While no one has heard of a nation being born in one day, God promises that very thing.

From this perspective, Isaiah 66:10–14 has a proleptic quality, that is, the passage invites the congregation to rejoice in the present as if the future restoration has already happened. In a limited way the community can live in the present as if the future is here. Verses 10–11 picture Jerusalem as a nursing woman and invite the congregation to rejoice at the coming of the restoration as at the birth of an infant.

In verses 12–14, the feminine reference shifts so that God is now the mother comforting the child (the community). In the new world, Jerusalem will prosper and enjoy security akin to that of a nursing infant (v. 12). A key feature is that the nations (Gentiles), having seen Judah's witness (Isa. 55:3–4), will be in such solidarity with Judah that the wealth of the nations will support the community. In a proto-apocalyptic touch, the prophet foresees the bodies of the faithful flourishing like grass in the new world, whereas God will come with fire and will angrily slay those who have not cooperated with the divine purposes (vv. 14–16).

The aim of this text is to help the congregation develop the confidence to live through struggle toward inclusive well-being. Nevertheless, the proto-apocalyptic element in the text introduces two issues. For one, the promise of divine intervention is an expression of covenantal faithfulness, *hesed*, and is the means toward ultimate inclusive well-being. If the preacher expects such an intervention, the preacher can simply apply this text directly to the congregation. However, if the preacher does not believe God will singularly intervene in history, the preacher could help listeners identify ways in which the congregation and culture are struggling toward blessing. How is the situation of the congregation and the culture like that of a woman in labor? How can the congregation join God in the struggle for blessing?

The other issue is the harsh picture of judgment in verses 14b–16. The preacher should wrestle with the congregation regarding whether they believe that God will come in flames of fire to slay the wicked. As noted earlier, this picture seems to me a contradiction of the network of convictions that God acts out of *hesed* in seeking inclusive well-being and in keeping covenant. I would thus offer a theological corrective to this part of the text.

Hosea 11:1–11 (Proper 13)

Hosea spoke prior to the exile, during the eighth century B.C.E. when Israel violated the covenant by worshipping Baal (e.g. 2:2–23; 4:4–19). Moreover, Assyria threatened Israel. After the monarch Jereboam II died (746 B.C.E.), several leaders attempted to seize power. Violence and assassinations were rampant (7:3–7), as were foolish and unfaithful alliances with other nations (7:11) and even relying on Israel's own military might (8:14). Ethical violations took place in everyday dealings (e.g. 4:2–3; 12:7–9). Consequently God was punishing Israel (9:1–10:15). However, repentance was possible (e.g. 14:1–7). Hosea 11:1–11 falls into three sections.

1. Verses 1–4 recall the formative history of God and Israel. In v. 1, God says that God loved Israel when Israel was a child, as we can see in the fact that God called Israel from Egypt (v. 1). For its part, Israel

abandoned God by worshipping Baals (v. 2). However, no matter
how flagrant the child's disobedience, God continued to be the
faithful parent. Indeed, verses 3–4 describe God and Israel having
an intimate parent-child relationship: God teaches Ephraim (Israel)
to walk, holds the community in God's arms even when the
community did not recognize God, lifted Israel to God's cheek, and,
like a mother, bent to feed Israel.

2. Following the covenantal model in which disobedience leads to curse,
   verses 5–7 set out the consequences of the child's disobedience.
   When the people failed to repent, Assyria overran Israel, and Israel's
   social world became a chaos.

3. Verses 8–11 reveal God's ultimate purposes. Yes, Israel will suffer the
   consequences of disobedience. However, punishment is only the
   penultimate experience. God's parental compassion shapes His
   future behavior. God will not make Israel like Admah and Zeboiim—
   cities God devastated (v. 8a–b; cf. Deut. 29:23). The thought of
   complete destruction causes God's heart to recoil. Instead, God feels
   compassion, which is the capacity to feel the situation of another and
   to respond in light of the best interests of the other. God feels tenderly
   toward Israel (v. 8c). Israel does suffer, but only enough to learn its
   lesson. God could respond to Israel with "fierce anger" that would
   destroy the people. While a human ruler might instinctively destroy
   Israel, this God responds, not like a retributive mortal, but from the
   perspective of a fully mature parent who ultimately wants what is
   best for the child (v. 9).

The passage ends with God roaring like a lion who has the power to
restore the community (v. 11a). The people tremble like children, like birds,
when God brings them home. They anticipated the full onslaught of God's
destroying anger, and so are initially hesitant to believe God's expression
of divine compassion (vv. 11b–12).

A sermon could encourage the congregation to take responsibility
for ways that we violate covenant. This text is, then, both a warning and
an assurance. The warning is that we will suffer the consequences of our
disobedience. The assurance is that God does not abandon us to destruction.
Like a compassionate, covenant-keeping parent who operates out of *hesed,*
God is always present to urge us to repent and to help us re-create our
worlds in faithful ways.

A preacher could develop the sermon around parent-child imagery.
Indeed, as a parent I often ache for our children in the most poignant
ways. While parent-child language could be evocative for many in the
congregation, it could also alienate adults who do not have children or
whose parents were dysfunctional. The preacher would want to provide
portals through which such folks could enter the sermon.

The preacher might also help the congregation recognize ways that we, like Israel, hesitate to accept God's unconditional love for us. I have heard people say, both directly and indirectly, "It seems too good to be true." No wonder since we, too, tremble like children and birds.

Sermon Series That Help the Congregation Realize Who God Is Not

Preachers who do not follow the lectionary have the freedom to create sermon series that can use several sermons to explore particular topics in more depth than is typically accommodated by a single text or to focus on texts or topics that do not occur in the lectionary.[16] I propose two such sermon series here, one based on biblical texts and another based on theological topics. Both relate to the central theme of this chapter—clarifying who God is not.

A Series Based on Biblical Texts

This series identifies four texts that represent ways in which people often think of God in the Torah, Prophets, and Writings. Each sermon might contain (a) an exposition of the text, (b) a theological critique that shows how the text is in conflict with the preacher's deepest convictions concerning God, and (c) a clear and theologically informed alternative. Where possible, the preacher can discern the underlying purpose of the text and note how this purpose does not depend on theologically objectionable elements in the text. These texts are not found in the Revised Common Lectionary.

1. Amos 2:1–16. This text asserts that God will punish Moab and Israel. However, from my point of view, God does not directly destroy communities in the way that Amos says that God will send fire on Moab and will orchestrate Israel's military defeat. We may bring those consequences on ourselves, but when we do, God is always working with us for restoration.
2. Psalm 137:7–9. This passage is prayer for Israelites to be happy when they dash the babies of their enemies against the rock. However, I do not believe God is pleased with killing innocent people, not even the infants of our enemies.
3. Job 1:6–21. God allows Satan to test Job. God does not inflict pain on us in order to test us in the way that God made a bet with Satan that allowed Satan to destroy Job's life as a test of Job's faithfulness.
4. Deuteronomy 28:1–6, 15–19. This passage assumes that God gives material blessing to the obedient and curses the material lives of the disobedient. However, life reveals cases in which the obedient suffer and the disobedient prosper.

A Topical Series

In a topical sermon, the preacher does not center the sermon in the exposition of a text but offers a theological interpretation of a topic from the perspective of the preacher's theology. The preacher may make use of the Bible, historic and contemporary Christian doctrine, and other sources.[17] This series would consider behaviors or attributes that Christians sometimes attribute to the God of Torah, Prophets, and Writings. Each sermon would focus on how Christians sometimes misperceive God. Each sermon below could contain three parts: (a) an explanation of the misconception, (b) a theological critique, and (c) a positive alternative.

1.   God does not have a split personality: wrathful (Old Testament) and loving (New Testament). In both parts of the Bible, God both judges and loves; indeed, God's judgment is often an expression of God's love.

2.   God is not an anal-retentive legalistic deity who makes us obey commandments to earn God's love. In all sections of the Bible, God is fundamentally a God of grace who looks upon us with unmerited favor.

3.   God is a not a super-sized abusive male (whose maleness and brutal behavior authorizes the superiority of human males and their brutal treatment of others). We speak about God anthropomorphically and metaphorically, but God is beyond gender and seeks a world in which women and men are egalitarian partners.

4.   God is not just our private benefactor who only blesses those who believe in God–Christians (and perhaps Jewish people). God seeks to bless all people.

5.   God does not directly inflict chaos and suffering on people and nature. While we may bring such circumstances on ourselves, God is ever with us to help us make our way toward repentance, repair, and renewal.

Over the seasons of preaching, a minister hopes to help the congregation feel increasingly less like they are being sent to the principal's office and more like they are in the presence of the faithful, covenant-keeping God who seeks their entire well-being.

3

It Seemed Like a Good Idea at the Time: Character Flaws in the Old Testament

MARTHA MYRE

I grew up learning about the "Great Heroes of the Bible." I heard how Abraham was the righteous man responding in faith to God's call. I heard how Jacob was the father of the twelve sons who became the twelve tribes. I heard about Joseph who saved not only his own people from starvation but the whole great land of Egypt. I heard how Moses argued with Pharaoh and was the instrument by which God brought God's people out of slavery. And then there was David fighting Goliath with only a few stones and a whole lot of faith. Wow! What amazing men. What paragons of faith! Even as children these figures loomed large.

What wasn't clear to me was how these ancient men had any relevance for a nine-year-old girl. I wasn't going to leave my father's house; I wasn't going to lead people out of slavery. I didn't think that I could be as noble as Joseph when his brothers' jealousy led to his slavery. I wasn't aware of any giants that needed slaying, and I was terrible with a slingshot.

Not until I was in my thirties and in Disciple Bible Study[1] did I actually read the stories for myself all the way through. What a revelation! These men were emphatically not heroes. Abraham left the promised land almost as soon as he arrived, and then he sold his wife to Pharaoh (Gen. 12:10ff). Jacob was a liar and a cheat and caused terrible problems among his wives and children with his favoritism. Joseph was an annoying little braggart who eventually was responsible for enslaving the entire Egyptian populace (see particularly Gen.47:13–26). Moses was a murderer and complainer. And David was a self-serving adulterous murderer. Turns out these guys were really interesting. And there were women as well: Sarah, who counted with God even if Abraham didn't think so; Rebecca, who was clever and forceful; Tamar, who was brave and resourceful; the women of Exodus 1, who completely thwarted the Egyptian king's plans; Miriam, who taught the people of God how to celebrate God's victory (even if she was a bit bloodthirsty); Rahab, who may have been a Jericho whore but had more faith in Yahweh than the Israelite people. These were people who jumped out from the pages of an ancient book as real and vital. They were not the perfect, righteous people of my childhood Sunday school class, but they had something to say to me. Amazingly enough. it was these wildly imperfect people whom God used in the divine plan to save the world from evil.

The title of this chapter is "It Seemed Like a Good Idea at the Time," and we shall see how that could be the motto of many of the characters in the Hebrew Bible. But I have to think that this could also be a line that God might have used. (In fact, the text says something like that in Genesis 6:6, "And the LORD was sorry that he had made humankind on the earth, and it grieved him to his heart.") This chapter will describe how character flaws and bad judgment by Old Testament figures, though they lead to bad consequences, are, after the fact, redeemed by God's grace and woven into the tapestry of the story of divine redemption. These stories enable us to see our own flaws for the purposes both of forgiving ourselves for our mistakes and learning to make better decisions. Just as God redeems mistakes in the Old Testament by weaving them into the plan of salvation, so God redeems our flaws and mistakes.

Flaws, Failures, and Grace

In the *Star Wars* movie series, the line, "It's not my fault!" becomes a kind of meme. However, George Lucas is simply using to humorous advantage one of the character flaws that humans have had from the beginning. As we will see in more detail in the exegesis portion of this chapter, the first man and woman are natural-born buck-passers. But probably the most difficult and ubiquitous flaw that we see is the desire to replace God, particularly to replace God with self. This desire to do what is right in our own eyes is clearly at the heart of the human condition.

God is not to blame for this, but the creation narrative suggests the reason for our desire to be like God. We are created in the image and likeness of God and given dominion over the rest of the created world, under the wise rule of God. God's hand has formed us, and God's very breath enlivens us. We are created to be a part of the body of Christ. So with all of that, it is no wonder that we think we are something special. But throughout the

Old Testament, humankind has forgotten, over and over, that in order to be formed into the image of God, we must be in relationship with God.

Take that first couple. Happy in their beautiful garden...until the woman decides that a snake knows better than God. Their decision to go their own way must have seemed like a good idea at the time. But the mistakes do not end with the first generation. Generation two is responsible for the first murder. Cain, in his older brother desire to be placed above his younger brother, to be the one noticed, makes sure that his younger brother will no longer be noticed because he will no longer be living. But just as God was gracious to his parents, God is bafflingly gracious to Cain. Though Cain has introduced murder to the world, God shows no signs of desire to give Cain what we would probably see as his "just deserts." Instead of putting Cain to death as punishment, God puts on him a mark of protection. The real punishment is that the earth will no longer be fruitful for Cain (Gen. 4:12–13); he will have to reassess his purpose in life. He becomes a builder of cities instead of a tiller of the ground (Gen. 4:17).

Even in the Noah story, although God wipes the world clean of the evil that has taken hold, God does not give up on the life that He has created. God saves Noah and family, along with the animal population over which humankind is supposed to rule. However, God discovers that the cleansing plan has not worked because "the inclination of the human heart is evil from youth" (Gen. 8:21). In fact, sin or evil is "original" to every human being. Perhaps a better word would be intrinsic. So God promises never again to bring destruction upon the earth, at least by means of a flood. Since this way of ridding the world of evil has not been able to touch the evil in the heart of humans, God begins the long plan of redemption that starts with Abraham and ends with Jesus.

But of course, that evil in the human heart affects all of those that God calls and uses. Each of the patriarchs that are often held up to Sunday school children as models of faith has a distinct problem. Abraham, and each of his descendants after him, proves to be unsuited for the burden of the covenant that God makes with him. Upon close examination, these men and women don't seem ideal for the carrying of a covenant that will be God's answer to sin and evil in the world. And yet, God continues to honor, to remember that covenant. In this chapter, we will take a look at each of these Genesis patriarchs (and at least a bit at the matriarchs), as well as Moses and David. We will see how each of these "great" men and women expresses both the human condition of sin and faithfulness to God.

Abraham does not begin as a righteous man. He begins simply as one who answers the initial call of God. But Abram is determined to make his own way. Is it possible that we should understand him as one who answered the call of God to escape the dominance of his father? Abram shows his desire for doing things his way almost immediately after arriving at the promised land. At the first sign of trouble—a famine in the land—he goes down to Egypt. Abram seems to have no recognition that he needs his wife to be fruitful. He virtually sells her to Pharaoh because he is fearful of his own life. Instead of relying on the protection of God to save him and his wife from the Pharaoh's perceived lustful eye, he misleads the Egyptian king into thinking that Sarai is fair game for his harem. In putting his wife at risk, Abram puts the covenant at risk. Abram continues to show disregard for the covenant promises as he offers the best land to his nephew, Lot, when they are forced to divide their households (Gen. 13:9). And he is more than willing to try his wife's solution to the problem of barrenness—take to bed his wife's Egyptian slave, Hagar. Abram's continued attempts to arrange for the fulfillment of the covenant continue to cause that covenant to be put at risk and cause dissension among his household.

God begins to make real progress in the forming of a righteous man when, on the one hand, God establishes authority over Abraham through the requirement of circumcision (Gen.17:10) and the name change and, on the other hand, gives Abraham the authority to question God's actions (Gen. 18:17–19). Not until Abraham reflects on God's righteousness does he begin to develop his own. God has trusted Abraham with his plan for Sodom; Abraham is later able to trust God with God's plan for the covenant, even when it appears that God is the one putting the covenant at risk by demanding the life of Abraham's son (Gen. 22).

Unlike his father, who keeps trying to take control, Isaac has the opposite flaw. Isaac abdicates responsibility for the covenant, leaving that to his wife Rebecca. Being almost sacrificed seems to have made Isaac a passive character who is found lying on his deathbed a good 20 years before he actually dies (Gen. 27; 35:28). However, Rebecca is the spiritual child of Abraham and is determined in her own right to arrange for her favorite son to be the covenant-carrier. Her actions lead to the effective loss of both sons, as Jacob is forced to leave home to avoid the murderous anger of his wronged brother, and Esau leaves home to marry the wrong woman (Gen.28:9).

Jacob's deceit is the least of his flaws. More importantly, he continues the family tradition of trying to control God. In fact, wrestling defines Jacob's whole life. He wrestles with his brother for control of birthright and paternal blessing. After God has already offered a blessing to Jacob, Jacob attempts to wrest control of their relationship in Genesis 28:20–22: "Then Jacob made a vow, saying, 'If God will be with me, and will keep me in this way that I go, and will give me bread to eat and clothing to wear, so that I come again to my father's house in peace, then the LORD shall be my God, and this stone, which I have set up for a pillar, shall be God's house; and of all that you give me I will surely give one tenth to you.'" Jacob literally wrestles for control in the text that bookends his sojourn with Laban (Gen.

32:24). Despite the fact that Jacob is involved in a power struggle with God, God continues to bless Jacob, recreating him as Israel, the one who wrestles with God and prevails. But in prevailing over his wrestling partner, Jacob is both permanently wounded and somehow changed. His whole life has been about grabbing for things, but after wrestling with God, he is able to experience the presence of God in the company of his previously estranged brother.

The last of the Genesis patriarchs, Joseph, begins as a spoiled boy, doted on by his father and hated by his brothers. Yes, he has dreams that God sends to him; but in sharing those dreams he all but guarantees that his brothers will be consumed by jealousy. Though Joseph is presented as a righteous and pious man—turning down the advances of his master's wife, attributing his success to God—he is still beset by the family flaw. He does things his own way. Instead of simply blessing the Egyptian people with grain during the famine, he forces them to buy their own grain back from him with money, livestock, land, and finally, themselves. Joseph is a mixed blessing to the Egyptian people. He provides food, but he also enslaves the whole population (except for the priests) for Pharaoh. Does the Egyptian Pharaoh of Exodus fame decide to enslave the Israelite people because they are the only free people in the land of Egypt?

A candidate for the most important figure in the Old Testament is Moses. He is the one who leads the people out of slavery, the one who gives the law. In terms of biblical heroes, he probably qualifies, yet he too has his issues. In trying to right a wrong—an Egyptian task-master whipping a Hebrew slave—Moses becomes a murderer. In the archetypal call story, Moses expresses his feelings of unworthiness. However, his claims of being "slow to speech" are called into serious question by the length and depth of his argument with God. One gets the feeling that Moses simply doesn't want the task that God seems determined to give him. With all of Moses' whining and excuses, God is patient and has a response, accommodating Moses' worries. And perhaps a reluctant Moses is far better than one who is eager for the job. He is forced to rely on God at every step of his journey with the people of Israel. He also plays a large part in changing the mind of God when God once again wants to destroy God's creation (Ex. 32:7ff). This time it is the creation of the people of Israel that God looks to destroy, for much the same reasons as God sent the flood: The people are corrupt and worship false idols. God would make of Moses a sort of new Noah, destroying all the descendants of Abraham and starting over with Moses. And yet Moses has developed enough wisdom to remind God of God's promises.

The excuse of Aaron to Moses in explaining the making of the golden calf must rank as one of the funniest of the biblical narratives as he proves once again that people are buck-passers: "I threw the gold in the fire and out came a calf!" (Ex. 32:24). Indeed. And Moses proves once again that human beings, including those carrying the covenant, want to be in control. Having persuaded God to pardon the people, Moses punishes them himself (Exod. 32:27, where it is not clear that God was the one who ordered the Levites to kill the sinners).

Before moving to the last of our "Great Heroes of the Bible," King David, let's take a moment to consider the books of Joshua and Judges. Judges in particular reflects a continuing cycle of the people turning away from God and going their own way. And at each turn, God is merciful. God listens to the cry of God's people and sends a leader to save them. Reading through the Bible with my eight- and ten-year-old daughters, I was fascinated by their comments: "Why didn't God ever learn that these people weren't worth saving? That they would disappoint God over and over? Why did God keep forgiving them?" The book of Judges ends with rape, murder, fratricide (in the form of warring tribes), and the utter devastation of women and children. All because "Every man did what was right in his own eyes." And yet, once again, God gives the people what they think they need and want—a human king to rule over them and fight their battles for them.

Incredibly, the king that is known as the "man after God's own heart" (1 Sam. 13:14) is yet another scoundrel. Even in his epic battle against Goliath, where he expresses faith in the God of Israel, David also is clearly fighting in order to win the girl and half the kingdom, so to speak (1 Sam. 17:25–26). He becomes both an adulterer and a murderer and is unable to keep peace in his own household among his sons, who engage in rape, murder, and political intrigue. And yet, even though he is far from perfect, David does have one redeeming feature: unlike other kings of Israel and Judah, including his own son Solomon, David never leads the people away from the worship of Israel's God.

Hope for Ourselves

As preachers, what do we do with these rascals, scoundrels, liars, and lawbreakers? We really don't want people to emulate their behavior, at least, not most of it! But I want to suggest that it is precisely because these biblical folk are so imperfect and, well, human, that they present us with great opportunity to preach grace. Contrary to popular opinion, the God of Israel really is the same as the God we know in Jesus. And, if we read carefully and without our rose-colored, Sunday school glasses, we will see the patience, grace, forgiveness, and steadfast love of God who works with the people he has. We are able to see how Abraham grows into the role that God prepares for him. How Jacob wrestles with becoming a fit carrier of the covenant and eventually prevails. We realize that even those closest to God have moments of doubt and failure. And in those realizations, we find hope for ourselves.

Genesis 3:8–15

I find it fascinating that many people blame Adam and Eve for all their problems. My mother used to say (with exasperation), "I am going to have to talk to Eve when I get to heaven about why she ate that apple!" The implication is that if Eve hadn't eaten that apple, then childbirth wouldn't be so difficult. If Eve hadn't eaten that apple, then we would still be in Paradise. Really? Seriously? The point of "original" sin is that it is original to each one of us, *not* that the sin of Eve and Adam was *the* original sin. We *all* are sinners and have fallen short of the glory of God (Rom. 3:23). The story of the first man and woman is the story of every person who has ever lived. In fact, that sort of attitude–blame it on Eve (and maybe Adam, too)–just highlights the point of this story: we are all buck-passers. Why blame ourselves for our sin if we can blame the "original" man and woman?

But there is more to this story than the obvious one of whom to blame. Not only the flaw of guilt, but a number of other weaknesses and flaws play roles in this text. If we look at the passage leading up to this text, we can see that when we last left the garden all was well. God is pleased with creation. Man and woman are pleased with each other. Life is good. For about ten minutes! Then the woman commits the first of several blunders–she listens to a snake. As one of my professors used to say, "One should *never* listen to a talking snake!" She listens because the snake is crafty or clever. The Hebrew word for this (*arum*) does not necessarily indicate that one is crafty in a bad way; it is used in Proverbs of people who are clever as opposed to those who are fools (cf. Prov. 12:16, 12:23, 13:16). The word *arum* is similar to the word for "naked" that we have in 2:25, so there might be a word play here. Furthermore, serpent or snake is not identified with Satan in Genesis. Later on the snake came to be seen as Satan or a tool of Satan because the snake does what the Satan (or *HaSatan*, which just means "Accuser") always does: he misleads by telling only a part of the truth. In this case, this clever snake asks what appears to be a simple question: "Did God say that you may not eat from any tree in the garden?" God, of course, said no such thing. In fact, God gave the trees to the person specifically to eat, with the exception of one tree, which was forbidden.

Having committed an error of judgment in listening to the snake, the woman falls into a much more serious mistake–she *answers* the snake. She can perhaps be forgiven for listening to the snake; perhaps he is simply a new voice to hear. However, in answering, the woman rushes to God's defense. In modern psychological parlance, she allows herself to be triangled[2] into whatever quarrel the snake may have with God. Not having family therapist Edwin Friedman as a coach, she doesn't know that the correct answer (if answer is even needed) would be, "Take that up with God." Instead, she defends the one who never needs defending: We *may* eat the fruit from the trees in the garden. Only the tree in the middle of the garden is forbidden.

And here she adds to God's words (some have called this the first sin), "We may not even touch it!" Of course, God has said nothing about touching it. This presents an obvious dilemma: What does she mean by saying "God told us not even to touch it?" Is she "projecting," knowing that if she touches it she is likely to taste it? Or does the woman believe that God is not quite up to defending Godself, and moreover, God's commandment is not quite up to snuff? This changing of the words of God indicates a slight under-confidence in God, a hint of the attitude that "If *I* had given a commandment, this is what *I* would have said."

Having spotted a crack in the woman's faith in God, the snake goes on to say that by eating the fruit of the tree in the middle of the garden the man and woman can be "like divine beings who know good and bad" (Tanakh). This appeals to the woman. From the slight hint that the woman knows better than God, we are now in full-blown "Let me run the universe" mode. She wants to be like God or like a divine being. And she makes yet another mistake–she believes that knowledge is the key to being Godlike.

The woman sees that this forbidden tree is great to look at, seems to have extra-delicious fruit, and has the added benefit of making one wise. So from that small beginning of listening to a suspicious voice, through the path of thinking her answer better than God's and desiring to *be* like God, she takes that final step: She chooses to believe the word of a snake over the word of God; she takes the fruit and eats. But this full-fledged sin of direct disobedience is the logical outcome of all of those small steps away from God. And where is her husband in all this? Why, he has been standing there alongside her all the time. So she hands him the fruit and he, too, eats.

This act of giving and taking shows an interesting dynamic in the relationship between the man and the woman. They have been created to be suitable partners for each other, to help one another live lives of fulfillment, to be protectors of and saviors for each other. But in this exchange of fruit, they not only break the relationship with God, they break relationship with each other. The woman is the one who does all the talking to the snake. She is the "dominant" partner here, but unfortunately, she is not fulfilling the role of a "suitable" partner. Instead, she leads him into disobedience. He, on the other hand, has not objected at any point, either to her addition to the words of God or to her taking of the fruit (or to her conversation with a snake!). In seeking to be "like gods," the man and woman have damaged the most godlike part of themselves–the part that is in relationship with God and with each other.

After they eat, "the eyes of both were opened." Now, generally in the Bible, having one's eyes opened is a good thing. However, this time it leads to a sad consequence. Now they can see that they are vulnerable, and it worries them, so they cover themselves with fig leaves (maybe a joke here–lots of folks are allergic to fig leaves). When they hear God walking in the garden, as God is evidently used to doing, they are afraid for the first time and hide themselves. In one sense, it is appropriate for the man and woman to fear or be in awe of God. And yet, this is a new behavior for them. The balance between reverence for and friendship with God has been upset. When God questions them as to their presence, they reply with one of the saddest statements in the Bible: We heard you were here, but we hid. Perhaps even more than the direct disobedience, this statement is a sign of the deep flaw in humanity. To know the presence of God and yet to hide from that presence is surely a source of pain for the God who, with deep compassion, saw that being alone was a bad thing for a human being (cf. Gen. 2:18). Now God is essentially alone in the garden–no longer in close relationship with the beings who were created with care and enlivened with God's own breath.

God, of course, knows what has happened, but instead of a direct confrontation, He questions the couple. And here is where we see what humans have become through their increasing reliance upon their own judgment instead of upon the words of God: buck-passers. Just as we are today, both the man and the woman are ready to point the finger of blame at someone else. So when God questions the man, who does the man blame? Look carefully now. The traditional answer that you learned in Sunday school is that the man blames the woman (as did my mother!). But the primary one is that the man blames is God! "You gave me the woman, God, so you are responsible!" When God turns the questioning on the woman, she blames the snake. Both humans blame someone else: "It's your fault, God!" or "The devil made me do it!" (if I can be forgiven for temporarily importing the Christian view of the snake). Neither owns up to his or her mistake.

I will say it again: The story of the first man and woman is the story of every person who has ever lived save one: Jesus. We would so love to blame them for our troubles, but it just won't wash. We are still listening to surrounding voices in preference to the voice of God. We still think we can do things better than God, that we are smarter than God. We are responsible for our own sins, and until we realize that, God cannot begin a new creation in us.

If we are to get all the way to redemption in this story, we must go further than the lectionary text. It covers only the "punishment" of the snake. But, despite the fact that we often speak of God's words to the man and woman as punishment, they are, in fact, no such thing. They are the natural consequences of what the two humans have asked for. They wanted to know what it was like to be gods, what it was like to understand both good and evil, so God gives them that knowledge. No longer is fruitfulness easy for them; now they will each be fruitful only through great struggle. No longer will they have a relationship defined by comfortable vulnerability with each other and with God; now they will live in fear of one another and of God. The partnership with the animal world is broken as well, as animals become not a source of companionship but a commodity to be used for the comfort of humans.

The story of what we call the "fall" sets up the long problem of evil to which much of the rest of the biblical narrative responds. Despite being made in the image of God, despite being shaped and formed by God's own hand, despite being enlivened by the very breath of God, humanity has deep flaws that will be the source of immense suffering and pain, not only for humanity itself but for God. In the end, it is the identification of God with and the suffering of God on behalf of these frail, flawed humans that will bring redemption to all of creation. To be "like" God is to share in the long, difficult work and suffering. God gives us what we ask for. If we ask for the wrong thing, we have only ourselves to blame.

Genesis 17:1–17

This is the third of three passages that relate to the covenant God makes with Abraham. The first is the passage in 12:1–4, which is the original call of Abram. God calls Abram to leave his family and go where God directs in order that his family may become, through the long years, a blessing to the families of the earth. The second covenant story is the passage in chapter 15, which includes the much-quoted passage, "Abram believed God and it was reckoned to him as righteousness." Here we see a covenant ceremony reminiscent of ancient Near Eastern rituals. God makes the covenant, and despite being the more powerful participant, places Godself in the position of being the primary keeper of the covenant (by passing through the cut animals in the guise of the smoking fire pot and flaming torch.) In the first passage, Abram's only necessary response is to follow where God leads. In the second passage, Abram responds with "belief" but little more. Not until this third passage is a concrete response required of Abraham.

Though the three passages are considered from three different sources, in the final form of the text they are a cumulative statement about the nature of the covenant between God and this prototype of God's people. Just as Adam is the original sinner, Abraham is, in a sense, the original solution to the problem of sin. However, Abram hasn't done a great job of bringing blessing to the families of the earth. God has given him land, promised him fruitfulness. But Abram gives up the land at the first sight of trouble, going to Egypt almost as soon as he arrives in the promised land. He gives up land again to his nephew Lot, telling him to choose whatever he wants. As for fruitfulness, Abram clearly doesn't think Sarai is a necessary component of this: He sells her to a foreign king twice, and he takes a household slave as a concubine in order to have a child by her. He is not even able to provide for shalom in his own household, between his women. Abram does not, at first blush, seem to be the righteous man idealized by the New Testament writers.

What Abraham gives up when he follows God's call is not, as I used to think, everything in his life. He takes with him his wife, his nephew, his household, and all his possessions. What he leaves behind is his heritage: his place in the world, the knowledge of who he is, and how he fits. He gives up his reliance on the traditions of his family in order to depend on this God who has called. But he clearly does not find reliance on God an easy thing. We throw around the phrase that "God doesn't call the equipped, God equips the called." And in this case, it is true. God has to work with Abram to form him into a person who can carry the weight of the covenant. The "training of Abram" takes place through the call of chapter 12 and the covenant ceremonies in 15 and 17. It continues when God allows Abraham to be a party to his decision to destroy Sodom, even allowing Abraham to question the divine judgment. It is not until God asks Abraham to sacrifice his beloved son, Isaac, that we know whether or not Abraham truly trusts the God who has called him.

In this third call/covenant passage, God has watched as Abram has attempted to have children in his own way–through the slave girl, Hagar. Perhaps because Abram uses his ability to reproduce inappropriately, God finally takes control of the organ of fruitfulness and thereby the process of fruitfulness. God is saying that *how* you reach the goal of the covenant– offspring without number–matters!

Abraham has tried to force God's covenant into his own conception of how fruitfulness will happen. He has taken a concubine in addition to his wife because he doesn't see that Sarah has a part in the covenant. This act of taking control leads to division and strife among the women of his household and eventually (if one follows the story to completion) to strife among the great nations fathered by his two sons–the sons of Ishmael and the sons of Isaac.

Once again, God promises that Abraham will have numberless children and be given the land. The covenant that God makes extends to Abraham's entire household; even the slaves and children of slaves born in his household are to be circumcised. This amazing inclusiveness is merely a first step in the long process of Abraham's family becoming a blessing. God also explicitly includes Sarai, now Sarah, in the covenant promise. This is a point that might be brought out in a sermon on this passage: The covenant is not solely for "Father Abraham" but also for "Mother Sarah" and, for that matter, all who reside in Abraham's household.

While the issue of control and forcing the covenant might be the main points in this passage, there is one more that would make interesting sermon fodder. The child who is born to Abraham and Sarah is named Isaac, "laughter." And he is named that for a good reason. When Abraham hears the covenant laid out before him, he falls on his face. We expect the text to say that he fell on his face and worshiped God. But instead he falls down laughing. Sarah laughs later, but Abraham laughs first. What does it mean to laugh at God when God makes promises? Is this really any better than hiding from God, as did the first man and woman? Humankind has progressed from hiding, to defying, and now to laughing at God. And this is the one who is God's answer to sin and evil! Once again, humankind's flaw becomes an opportunity for God's graciousness: Instead of punishing either or both Abraham and Sarah for their (potentially mocking) laughter, God simply gives them the promised son, and they name him Isaac, "laughter." Sarah's laughter has turned from the mocking laughter of disbelief to the joyful laughter of enjoying the fulfillment of God's promise.

2 Samuel 11:26–12:13

The third passage we will consider in the context of character flaws is that of David's self-condemnation. Uriah is dead because David has committed adultery with his wife and gotten her pregnant. The fruitfulness of David, far from being a blessing, is now a source of alarm and ultimately leads to death. David is unable to persuade Uriah to break with the demands of holy war and engage in sexual intercourse with his wife. So David simply has him murdered. In a way, it seems the perfect crime; because Uriah is abandoned to death in the middle of battle, his death cannot be directly and obviously traced to the actions of the king. Since David cannot be convicted in a court, God sends the prophet Nathan to trick David into convicting and condemning himself.

In preferring to call the woman Bathsheba "the wife of Uriah" instead of by her name, the text emphasizes David's adultery. She follows the appropriate rituals in making mourning for her husband before she is brought into the house of David as his wife. But this leads to the possibility of suspicion that either the child is not David's or the child is the result of adultery. Either way, this child will be a problem for David.

However, David has a larger problem: God is not pleased with him. The prophet Nathan comes to tell a story that we know to be a parable, but David believes it to be a literal description of a crime committed in his kingdom. As the righteous judge, David is angered by this clearly unrighteous behavior. He judges that the man deserves death and yet does not pronounce a sentence of death. Instead he hands down a sentence that displays mercy; the man will have to make fourfold restoration. When Nathan says to David "You are the man" and reveals that he is fully aware of the extent of David's sin, David does not make excuse. Instead, he acknowledges his guilt. As David has laid down a sentence of mercy, so does God. He does not ordain death for David, but the consequences of David's sin will still be severe. The child dies; though in the context of the story, the child could not be allowed to live for the reasons given above. David's house is in turmoil from that time on. His daughter is raped by his son. His concubines are used by his own son Absalom as tools to declare Absalom's usurpation of his father.

David has sinned greatly with the wife of Uriah. And yet, even here, God uses David's disobedience for his own purposes. The wife of Uriah becomes the mother of Solomon, the son who builds the temple and through whom the covenant will continue. God has once again used people who are deeply flawed to move forward God's plan of salvation.

Preaching Series

In preaching on these texts, the preacher must use caution. These are sacred texts and sacred people to many in our congregations. They will be resistant to seeing them as less than perfect. However, there are several ways to get around this problem. In discussing possibilities for sermon series, instead of simply providing a list, I will be suggesting topics and the questions you might ask yourself about those passages.

Using Texts Other Than Lectionary Texts

Dysfunctional Families of the Bible

One way of addressing these passages is to do a sermon series on "Dysfunctional Families of the Bible." Look into the research into family systems pioneered by Murray Bowen and popularized in the church by Edwin Friedman in *Generation To Generation: Family Process in Church and Synagogue* (The Guilford Press, 1985). The families of Genesis reveal how the "anxiety" is transmitted from one generation to the other, particularly in the stories of the first two generations and in the stories of how favoritism and jealousy move through the generations in the families of Abraham and later of David.

Adam and Eve, the first man and woman, are also the first dysfunctional family. A sermon focusing on the relationship between the man and woman could explore both the possibilities for companionship and partnership and how that partnership breaks down. Why does the man stand by as the woman is led into trouble by the snake? Is this a case of over/under functioning?[3] How does the relationship between the man and woman change because of their shared sin? If we blame only one of the pair (usually Eve), then aren't we ignoring the insight that it is the relationship that is in trouble?

The sons of Adam and Eve continue the dysfunction of their parents, showing the generational movement of anxiety. In the relationship between the brothers, where are the triangles? You might present Cain's murder of his brother as the ultimate form of "emotional distance."[4]

Continuing a look at the dysfunctional families, Abraham's family provides plenty of material. What generational patterns do you see? You can explore patterns of brother conflict, favoritism/jealousy, or deceit. In fact, these same patterns could be explored with fruitfulness in the stories of the family of David as well. If you present these people as having the same family issues as those in your congregation, your members can also be comforted and encouraged by the ways in which God continues to use them. God's mercy and remembering of the covenant is also a generational pattern!

The Many Faces of...

Another way to present these stories would be to help people see that these characters are not one-dimensional. A series on "The many faces of (insert favorite character)" could explore this idea. Abraham is presented as both a loving father and one who is willing to send one of his sons into the wilderness to die. He is a war leader in Genesis 14 (a passage not in the lectionary and rarely used but worth looking at). He is both a man of faith, going when God calls, and a man whose faith seems weak. Who is the "real" Abraham? David has many sides as well–lover, friend, warrior, king.

Character Flaws

An easy way to present both the flaws of the biblical characters and the grace of God would be to pick a particular flaw for specific characters and show the sin and the grace. For instance:

- Abraham: Look at his faithlessness and how God brings him to faithfulness.
- Isaac: Explore his inaction in comparison to Rebecca's action and how God uses both.
- Jacob: There are several possibilities here. Deceit is a theme in the life of Jacob. How does Jacob's deceit help or hinder the work of God? Or the theme of favoritism could be another focus.
- Joseph: Arrogance is a hallmark of Joseph. And yet he is also a model of forgiveness. What is the relationship between the two?
- Moses: Moses is a reluctant prophet, but one who eventually reminds a reluctant God of God's promises.
- David: Where to start! David is a man of passion. This causes him trouble when his passion is for women or power, but when his passion is for God, he becomes the one with whom God makes an everlasting covenant.

Using Lectionary Texts

Rethinking ...

If calling these families "dysfunctional" seems too harsh, you could simply call a series "Rethinking Genesis." In Year A of the Lectionary, we have texts from Genesis during the season after Pentecost. These texts include the stories that lift up the patriarchs as people of faith as well as the stories that show them in a less favorable light. Similarly, "Rethinking

Samuel" could be the series in Year B where the stories focus on David. Use these stories to contrast the positive characteristics of these men and women with darkness in their characters. In 2 Samuel 5:10 it says that "David became greater and greater, for the LORD, the God of hosts, was with him." But then a few weeks later we have the story of David's downfall.

The People of God–Flawed and Chosen

Instead of looking at individual characters, another way to present these texts as a series is to see both the flaws of and God's mercy toward the people as a whole. The first group that we see is found in Genesis 11, where the people have come together to build a tower reaching heaven. In this pivotal story the people try to make a name for themselves. But God scatters them and instead makes a name for Abraham. The books of Exodus, Numbers, and Deuteronomy are used in Year A and provide the opportunity for preaching on the people of God as a whole. In Exodus 1:8–2:10 the people have forgotten the source of their fruitfulness and strength. Exodus 3:1–15 tells of God's desire to save the people and make God's name known to them. In presenting Exodus 12:1–14, you could place it in the context of reminding the congregation that the people resisted God's plan to save them through Moses. Certainly the grumbling stories in Numbers 21:4b–9, Exodus 16:2–15, and Exodus 17:1–7 can be both a warning against grumbling and an example of God's provision, even for the people who are so ungrateful. The ten commandments or ten words found in the text of Exodus 20:1–4, 7–9, and 12–20 could be explored in the light of how these commandments both reveal our sins and highlight God's nature. Are these not given because these are the sins that define the human condition? But, on the other hand, these words define the values that are at the heart of the kingdom of God. Finally, we have that passage in Exodus 32:1–14 where we can explore the great irony of the people at the foot of the mountain creating for themselves a golden calf so they can have a visible representation of God. As they are breaking one of God's commandments, Moses has been on the mountain receiving from God instructions on making a tabernacle so that the presence and glory of God can be visible to and move with the people on their journey through the wilderness.

Closing Thoughts

These ideas should get you started. Looking at each preaching text, whether from the lectionary or not, in the context of the whole sweep of God's plan can help our congregations see themselves as a part of that plan and a part of the story of salvation. Remembering to bring out both the flaws of each character as well as the ways in which they followed and honored God can give hope to those who find faith a daily struggle. If you will read with the idea that these are not heroes of the faith but fallible human beings in need of grace, then you will not have to search for relevance; you will find it in abundance.

4

Sexuality and Eroticism in the Old Testament

By Mary Donovan Turner

In a sex-obsessed culture, how does the Old Testament enable us to achieve a healthier understanding of the place of sexuality in God's creation and in human relationships? Anyone with even a cursory understanding of the complexity of Old Testament history and literature knows this question is a daunting one. Sexual mores and norms are contextual; they are bound in culture, and the culture of the ancient near east is very different from our own. The understandings of sex and sexuality in the Old Testament, and in the New, revolve around values that are alien to most of us.[1] Can we use the Old Testament as a guide in this important conversation? What are our challenges? How do we use a text written in a time so vastly different from our own? Will we learn something new? Will something new be revealed when we study sexual mores from a different time and place? It is not enough that the Old Testament is filled with sex and innuendo. The Old Testament does not allow us to forget our sexuality; it is an important dynamic in the stories of our ancestors of faith. Neither does the Old Testament let us idolize it.[2] We must begin by identifying the challenges to Old Testament preaching on these subjects, and the themes and currents that informed ancient Israel's understanding of body, gender, and sexuality.

Beginning at the Beginning

Why don't we typically preach from Old Testament texts to learn and teach something about human sexuality? There are several varied, yet interrelated, reasons why this might be so.

47

1. Many of the stories that are sexual in nature are omitted in the lectionary. This enables the lectionary preacher to avoid them. A good example of this is the Old Testament book Song of Songs (or Songs of Solomon). In the Revised Common Lectionary, the Song of Songs appears only once and that is during the Ordinary Time, Proper 17, Year B. The eight short, sensual, and erotic chapters of Song of Songs are otherwise kept safely out of sight for the lectionary preacher.
2. Many of the stories in the Old Testament that are sexual in nature could evoke troubling and painful memories for the listeners who have known violence or been abused or traumatized.
3. There are often children present in worship, and the preacher doesn't want to broach subjects that may be uncomfortable and challenging for parents who would like to ignore or avoid questions related to sex.
4. Contemporary culture rarely treats sexuality in ways the church could affirm. Culture exploits sexuality and objectifies the body but represses discussion of sex in the contexts of love and commitment.
5. There is among Protestant clergy in many denominations and traditions a general lack of familiarity and comfort with the Old Testament text, which means that there is less preaching from the Old Testament in these communities in general.[3]
6. With the staggering amount of material that seminary training must cover, issues of sexuality are rarely addressed as an integral part of the curriculum. When these issues arise in pastoral counseling and other settings, ministers are often ill equipped to treat them in an informed way.
7. Pastors often feel reluctant to preach on the stories in the Old Testament that contain sexual elements, so they remain hidden. These stories typically contain incest, bigamy, mutilation, and rape (see Gen. 19, for example). Preachers may believe that these stories have little redemptive value and will confuse listeners. These stories need much explanation and many disclaimers. The church is not proud of this part of our heritage.
8. Texts like the story of Lot in Sodom have been misinterpreted, and have a deep and tenacious history in condemning homosexuality. This reflects and leads to misunderstanding on several levels: the personal, the interpersonal, the religious/social/educational, and the political. It may be difficult, then, for this population to be convinced that there is a conversation in the Old Testament that is both healthy and helpful.
9. The New Testament, because of the cultural and social environment in which it was birthed, advocates a radical split between body and spirit: the body being human and sinful, and the spirit being "of

God" and therefore good. This denigration of the "flesh" has discouraged the church to engage issues of the body and of a healthy sexuality.

Cumulatively, these comprise a huge wall, a barrier, for the preacher who would like to engage the subject of sexuality from the pulpit. Is it worth our while to climb over the obstacles and see what the Old Testament has to offer?

In Ancient Israel–Challenges in Understanding

A comprehensive survey of practices in ancient Israel in relation to gender and sexuality is not possible here. Yet, the identification of some of the more problematic aspects will demonstrate the difficulty of "transporting" Old Testament practices into contemporary, healthy practices. In ancient Israel sex was political, sometimes tied to war treaties, and definitely related to power. In the Old Testament, Moses encourages his men to use captured virgins for their own pleasure. After urging his men to kill male captives and female captives who are not virgins, he says, "But all the young girls who have not known man by lying with him, keep alive for yourselves" (Num. 31:18).[4] This implies that women were commodities, a spoil of war, property that could be bartered or won, used, and exploited after the last battle is fought and the goods are conquered or divided.

It is also true that "in the Old Testament, powerful men, the patriarchs, judges, and kings have sex with more wives; they have more sex with other men's wives; they have sex with more concubines, servants, and slaves; and they father many children."[5] This demonstrates again the important relationship between wealth, power, and the use of women. Stunning statistics demonstrate how this practice grew and developed. Abraham, the first patriarch, had two wives, Sarah and Keturah, and one concubine, Hagar. Centuries later Solomon was reported to have 700 wives and 300 concubines.[6] It is important to note the call for the patriarchs to be "fruitful and multiply." This call comes early in the creation story in Genesis 1; it is reiterated to Noah and then to Abraham as many as ten times! Sex was the avenue for fulfilling the calling from God to build the nation.

As a result of these kinds of understandings of sex, power, and control of women in the Old Testament, the narratives are permeated with accounts of women who are used and abused sexually by acquaintances, family members, and strangers. The brief synopsis below of selected stories from the Old Testament reminds us of the prevalence of these disturbing encounters:

1. **Genesis 18**–Lot throws his virgin daughters out into the crowd to satiate the men of the city who want the male visitors, the strangers, who were traveling through the city.
2. **Genesis 19**–Lot's daughters seduce him so they can be with child.

3. **2 Samuel 3**–King David's son Amnon conspired with a cousin to seduce Tamar, David's daughter and Amnon's half sister. When she would not consent to sex, he raped her, and then "hated her with a very great hatred."

4. **2 Samuel 2**–David calls for the beautiful Bathsheba and seduces her. When she becomes pregnant, David ultimately arranges for her husband to be murdered on the battlefield.

5. **Genesis 34**–While the Israelites were in Canaan, Dinah, daughter of Leah and Jacob, paid a call on the neighboring tribe, the Levites. Dinah was raped by a young nobleman, Shechem.

6. **Judges 19**–A Levite, his concubine, and servant were traveling from Bethlehem back to their homes in the hills of Ephraim. On the way they stayed in Gibeah and lodged for the night with an old Ephraimite they had met along the way. During the night, a mob calls for the Levite, but his host offers them the concubine instead. She is raped and dismembered.

Because women generally possessed less overt power, both physically and socially, their manipulation of sexuality to the harm of another often involves deception and subterfuge. Examples of this are Potiphar's wife, who wrongly accuses Joseph of rape and has him imprisoned; Delilah, whose accusations that Samson doesn't love her eventually leads him to disclose the basis of his phenomenal strength, making him vulnerable to the Philistines; and Tamar, who seduces her father-in-law who is trying to remove her from the family line.[7]

It is amazing that stories like those above are included in the national history of the Israelite people. Their raw honesty, their violence and brutality, are strongly woven into the narrative. What is their purpose? These stories are not intended to be prescriptive; they are *not* told as reminders of how life should be. They are, however, descriptive; they tell us how life is, interestingly in the ancient story and in our own. These stories are remembered and told as reminders of the ways that the nation "went astray." They are apologetically reminding the people how and when their ancestors lost their way.

Many of these stories carry within them a clue or a suggestion that these kinds of brutal acts are inconsistent with how life should be lived when in covenant with God. The David and Bathsheba story ends with the prophet Nathan telling an indicting parable that allows David to see and take account of his sinfulness. Judah says of his daughter-in-law, Tamar, "She was more righteous than I"–a testimony to his own waywardness. And the story of the Levite's concubine was a polemic to demonstrate how horrific things were in the land before Israel had a king and everyone did what was right in their own eyes.

A Sermon Series

There are several sermon series that might be considered when thinking about sexuality and eroticism in the Old Testament. These are interesting because these series would not grow comfortably out of New Testament texts. *It is the Old Testament that offers us these important opportunities.*

Sex Gone Awry

As we have witnessed, the Old Literature abounds in portraits of sexuality "gone awry." Certainly there is a place in preaching for us to name the places in our own societies where equally appalling things are happening as women, men, and children are abused by friends, family members, and strangers.[8] What are our responsibilities as ministers, priests, and pastors to name the realities of sexual and domestic abuse in our society and to help create a world that is safe and in which people do not live in fear?[9]

One sermon series could be structured around the laments of the Psalms; the psalmist cries out in despair because she/he is being tortured, abused, ridiculed, or forsaken. Who are these in our world? Whose cries are we called to hear? Consider the following:

> I am poured out like water, and all my bones are out of joint; my heart is like wax; it is melted within my breast; my mouth is dried up like a potsherd, and my tongue sticks in my jaws; you lay me in the dust of death. (Ps. 22:14–15 – Good Friday ABC; Proper 23, Year B)

> My tears have been my food day and night, while people say to me continually, "Where is your God?" (Ps. 42:3 – Easter Vigil ABC; Proper 7, Year C)

It is interesting that many of the cries of those who are being oppressed and abused are absent from the Lectionary (see for instance Pss. 6:6; 57:4; 17:13). A read-through the Psalms, however, will demonstrate that there is a strong and pervasive call to justice for the oppressed throughout its verses. This awareness opens new homiletic possibilities and allows entry into a conversation about those in our communities who are sexually abused.

The preacher could also consider a Lenten series that focuses on the world's lack of justice. Lent includes times of focused lament, confession, relinquishment, sacrifice, and repentance; the sounds of Lent are in a minor key. On Ash Wednesday, Year C, the Old Testament reading, Isaiah 58:1–12, invites us to such considerations. The prophet, unlike many preachers, will not allow us to be content with individualistic and personal, perhaps sentimental, Lenten thinking. As prophets do, Isaiah names the realities of life that he sees around him. He then interprets those realities in light of the people's relationship and covenantal commitment to their God. He is not satisfied with shallow devotion or empty ritual. There is an urgency in his voice. Chapter 58 begins, "Shout out …. Do not hold back …. Lift up your voice …. Announce …." There is no time to waste because the world suffers. God expects more than ashes on our foreheads and even penitent hearts. We are not simply to be focused on our personal, private redemption; we must be intent on public engagement, on mending the world. The prophet challenges us to replace poverty with care, compassion, and unconditional kindness; injustice with justice; and violence with reconciliation.

A sermon series on this kind of violence would allow us the opportunity to do theological formation within the community of faith. We could ask and answer questions such as: Why does God allow suffering? Where is God in these situations? What is our hope? What is radical and systemic evil? And what is forgiveness for the perpetrator? Is it required or even desirable?

How does the preacher prepare herself for preaching on this kind of issue? It takes more than learning the appalling facts and figures about the growing numbers of persons affected by this kind of violence. The following questions are helpful, even essential, for the preacher who addresses sexual and domestic violence from the pulpit:

- Does preaching on domestic violence bring it into the open in a way that will allow honest conversation and healing?
- Can we preach about domestic violence without having a system and network of care in place for those plagued with memories of their own abuse?
- How does the preacher bring a word that addresses both perpetrators and victims—both of whom will inevitably be a part of the community of faith?
- Is it ever appropriate for the preacher to name his/her own experiences of violence and abuse?
- How do we bring a word that will challenge the community to help bring forth systemic, political, and communal changes in our world?
- Are there other places (educational forums, etc.) where conversations about sexual abuse could more profitably take place?[10]

Sex and Pleasure

The second possibility for a sermon series is to focus on the need for pleasure, even sexual pleasure, and enjoying the creation God has given us. This is a sharp turn from the suggestion above, but, in some sense, may be equally challenging. Are there Old Testament texts that invite us to consider a healthy sexuality and that encourage us to see our passions as positive and even as gifts from God? Many of us have been programmed to believe that a faithful, God-driven life is one of suffering, one of scarcity and sacrifice.

There has been a recent effort to bring together conversations about spirituality and sexuality in an effort to counter a centuries-old assumption in the Christian community that our sexualities and our spiritualities are oppositional to each other. Influenced by the Greek traditions, Christianity has depicted sex as dangerous. Plato argued, for instance, that the only way a soul can gain freedom from temporary pleasures like sex is to redirect desire to beauty or truth or other "higher goods." The Stoic movement encouraged the cultivation of *apatheia*, the freedom from being moved by passion.[11] Thus there are passages in the New Testament, such as the following passage from Galatians, that have helped shaped early and subsequent Christian understandings:

> Live by the Spirit, I say, and do not gratify the desires of the flesh …. for what the flesh desires is opposed to the Spirit, and what the Spirit desires is opposed to the flesh; for these are opposed to each other, to prevent you from doing what you want…. Now the works of the flesh are obvious: fornication, impurity, licentiousness…. Those who belong to Christ Jesus have crucified the flesh with its passions and desires. If we live by the Spirit, let us also be guided by the Spirit. (Gal. 5:16–25)

Most of Christianity has been dominated by this kind of thinking. Early theologians, like Augustine, who set the foundation for Western Christian theology, linked unruly sexual desire to God's punishment for Adam and Eve's disobedience. Sex was necessary to perpetuate conception, but celibacy was holy and one of life's highest callings.[12]

Starting with the Protestant reformers, Martin Luther argued that sex was good for the soul, as important to life as drinking and eating. Still, he, Calvin, and Wesley argued strongly that the celibate, single life was spiritually preferable to marriage. And even now, at the beginning of the twenty-first century, the Roman Catholic church requires celibacy of its clergy, and other denominations and caucuses within denominations staunchly oppose various forms of sexuality.[13]

What does it mean, then, to redefine *eros,* to enlarge and expand our theological understandings in order to affirm it? Some are asking for and urging a wider concept of eros that would include not only the passion between lovers but also the sensual joy of many of life's activities and pleasures. Audre Lorde defines the "erotic" as *those physical, emotional, and psychic expressions of what is deepest and strongest and richest within each of us, being shared: the passions of love, in its deepest meanings.*[14] Many know passion through sexual relationships, or listening to music, or discovering new and provocative ideas, or sailing on the ocean waters. The word "erotic" is often viewed as a synonym for sexuality, but in the Greek the word includes not only the sexual but also intellectual, artistic, and spiritual yearnings. Many theologians have affirmed the power of *eros* as a central aspect of the Christian life.[15]

What happens, then, if we view our relationships with God, our spirituality, and our passionate relationships with others as related or symbiotic or interwoven? Can we reframe the wedge that has been driven between body and spirit by acknowledging a connection between our journey toward God and the journey toward coming to terms with our sexual embodiment?[16] This is important when most of our denominations and traditions are in conflict over varied manifestations of sexuality. Three texts are explored below. These could be used separately or in a series to explore the importance of creating among the listeners a positive appreciation for their passionate selves.

Any conversation about pleasure invites important ethical questions or considerations that must be foundational for any meaningful discussion about passion and pleasure. We know that the drive for pleasure and enjoyment can take on destructive expressions. How do we distinguish responsible pleasure and enjoyment from these destructive or abusive expressions?

Song of Songs 2:8–13 (Proper 9, Year A)

The Song of Songs is a collection of love poems; some say there are five poems, while others say there are as many as several dozen. The number of poems identified depends on the markers used to designate and divide one from another. The thread that runs through the poems and unites them is a conversation between a woman and a man. They express their love for one another; the imagery used is passionate and erotic. The lectionary reading for Proper 9, Year A from the second chapter of the Song of Songs is as follows:

> The voice of my beloved! Look, he comes, leaping upon the mountains, bounding over the hills. My beloved is like a gazelle or a young stag. Look, there he stands behind our wall, gazing in at the windows, looking through the lattice. My beloved speaks and says to me: "Arise, my love, my fair one, and come away; for now the winter is past, the rain is over and gone. The flowers appear on the earth; the time of singing has come, and the voice of the turtle dove is heard in our land. The fig tree puts forth its figs, and the vines are in blossom; they give forth fragrance.
>
> Arise, my love, my fair one, and come away. (Song 2:8–13)

Reading these verses in the context of the larger collection of poems, the reader begins to notice themes–threads that run through the whole. There is an excitement and urgency about finding and being with one another. There is longing. There is desire. The descriptions of their physical beauty are sensual and exotic. The hearing of each other's voices creates an anticipation of time that will be spent together. "Come and be with me!" is the repetitive cry.

There is a beauty here with which many, if not most, of the sermon listeners' can relate. It is about new and expectant and sexual love. Throughout the history of its interpretation in both Jewish and Christian communities, the Song of Songs was most often seen as an allegory or a depiction of the love between God and Israel in the former and God and the church in the latter.[17] These interpreters often insisted that the most passionate desire and love affair one can have is with God, the one who has created us. Song of Songs was seen as the kind of text that could help communities imagine what it is like to be in love with God—not a constant kind of ecstasy, but a searching and longing and finding of God who is sometimes elusive and distant. With this kind of interpretation, the Song of Songs was preached from more often than any other Old Testament book in the thirteenth century. The Song of Songs (and not the prophetic books) was one of the most often copied manuscripts of the Middle Ages.[18] The prophets Hosea, Jeremiah, and Isaiah also use the man-woman metaphor to depict the relationship between God and the community Israel, but in the prophets the relationship between man and woman, and God and community has gone awry. There is betrayal, anger, alienation, physical harm and abuse, and fear. In the Song of Songs there is delight; there is pleasure found in each other. If the Song of Songs was intended to be an allegory, which helps us understand the powerful and beautiful relationship between God and humanity, then it is significant that this alluring kind of sexual attraction and love was chosen to be used in this metaphorical or allegorical way. To be used as the metaphorical vehicle to describe our relationship with God bespeaks or implies a positive understanding of the human body and attraction.

Those throughout history who viewed the Song of Songs simply as a love song between two humans were sometimes named heretics and had their writings and interpretations burned. But beginning with the rise of the critical study of the Bible, the interpretations of the Song turned from the spiritual (a depiction of our relationship to God) to the physical (a description of the relationship between humans). The Song was compared to love lyrics in other cultures, and, interestingly, the Song's use in contemporary liturgies was consequently greatly diminished.[19]

An even more recent movement among biblical interpreters is not to choose the spiritual interpretation over the sexual, nor the sexual over the spiritual. This interpretation grants a rightful place to both spheres and sees an interplay between the two. The Song of Songs is seen as a celebration of eros—the relationship between two humans who seek out each other and know desire and who seek the connection that God has intended between humans when they were created for companionship. At another level this poem is about the strong desires we have for God as we search out and desire God. To see the poem as a celebration of both human and divine love blurs and makes ambiguous what is often seen as a strong divide between the sacred and the secular.[20] Can the passionate and human parts of our lives—our strong loving—be indicators of the life God wants us to live, not an apathetic but a robust and passionate engagement of the world God has created for us?

Genesis 2: 18–24 (Proper 22, Year B)

In contrast to the creation story in Genesis 1, the story in Genesis 2–3 focuses on our human situation. In chapter 2 we read an ideal description of the way life was intended to be for us. In chapter 3 we encounter our human embarrassments, struggle, alienation, and pain.

Preaching from Genesis 2 is difficult because listeners bring time-honored assumptions about the story to their hearing. Generations have heard that since man was created first, man is superior. Woman is created as "helper," which has wrongfully meant for interpreters that she is subordinate, dependent, derivative, and not an autonomous person. Man, on the other hand, has been seen as having the power and the right to rule over her. More recently this creation story has been used as a polemic against same-gender marriage since, as you may have heard, "Adam married Eve, not Steve." In this passage, however, helper is not intended to identify the woman as subordinate and dependent.[21] Indeed, the word "helper" is almost exclusively used in the Old Testament to describe God! And the story is not meant as a polemic against same-gender marriage; it is not about marriage at all![22] These skewed interpretations of the story distance us from the story's primary messages about the goodness of companionship and intimacy.

> Then the LORD God said, "It is not good that the man should be alone; I will make a helper as his partner." So out of the ground the LORD God formed every animal of the field and every bird of the air, and brought them to the man to see what he would call them; and whatever the man called every living creature, that was its name. The man gave names to all cattle, and to the birds of the air, and to every animal of the field; but for the man there was not found a helper as a partner. So the LORD God caused a deep sleep to fall upon the man, and he slept; then he took one of his ribs and closed up its place with flesh. And the rib that the LORD God had taken from the man he made into a woman and brought her to the man. Then the man said, "This at last is bone of my bones and flesh of my flesh; this one shall be called Woman, for out of Man this one was taken." Therefore a man leaves his father and his mother and clings to his wife, and they become one flesh. And

the man and his wife were both naked, and were not ashamed. (Gen. 2:18–25)

In this story, Adam, who is made from the dust of the earth, is given a companion, one who is suitable and fitting for him. Through the creation of the woman, male and female are created and given to one another. The male poetically responds to the gift of the female who is "bone of my bones and flesh of my flesh." He leaves father and mother and clings to the new creature and they become one flesh. Sexuality, *eros*, is given birth in this new creation.[23] There is no hint that male and female have a sexual relationship so that children can be birthed. Full humanity is found in community and relationship with one another. Sexuality is affirmed without qualification. It is neither the cause nor the result of the Fall. It is a part of God's good creation.

In our sex-obsessed culture in which healthy conversation is repressed, many negative and destructive messages are sent about our sexualities. How can the Genesis story be an antidote to the messages, stories, advertisements, and songs in our contemporary culture that depict abusive and devastating experiences that many have experienced? The story in Genesis 2 is one about mutuality, companionship, support, and engagement. How can the church be a part of promoting healthy, God-given sexualities?

Ecclesiastes 3:1–13 (New Year ABC), 2:18–23 (Proper 13, Year C)

Ecclesiastes finds its home, though not a completely comfortable one, in the Wisdom literature. Its title in Hebrew, Qohelet, is itself a mystery. Seemingly related to the word for "assembly," Qohelet is supposed to be a speaker to the gathering, a preacher. The speaker/author appears to be a man advancing in years who feels the weight of memory on his shoulders. What explains the inconsistencies he has seen during his lifetime? What is of importance? What is new? What endures? How do we understand the indiscriminate nature of suffering? He is not sure. He sees the injustices in the world around him but does not see that justice will ever prevail. People die. They are not remembered. The wealth they have accumulated will simply go to someone else who has not worked for it. And so he surmises that to eat and drink and find joy in one's toil is not only "as good as it gets" but is prescribed by God. Enjoy the world you have been given![24]

Only Ecclesiastes 2:18–23 and 3:1–13 have found their way into the Revised Common Lectionary, and although interpreters and commentators over the centuries have debated the book's value in the canon, it is often quoted and its poetry in chapter 3 has been put into song for the masses.

I hated all my toil in which I had toiled under the sun, seeing that I must leave it to those who come after me—and who knows whether they will be wise or foolish? Yet they will be master of all for which I toiled and used my wisdom under the sun. This also is vanity.

> So I turned and gave my heart up to despair concerning all the
> toil of my labors under the sun because sometimes one who has
> toiled with wisdom and knowledge and skill must leave all to be
> enjoyed by another who did not toil for it. This also is vanity and
> is a great evil. What do mortals get from all their toil and strain
> with which they roll under the sun? For all their days are full of
> pain, and their work is a vexation, even at night their minds do
> not rest. This also is vanity. (Eccl. 2:18–23)

The verse following this lectionary text reads, "There is nothing better
for mortals than to eat and drink, and find enjoyment in their toil. This
also, I saw, is from the hand of God." Initially Qohelet believes that even
the pleasures of drinking wine, eating, and sex (2:8) are also vanity and a
useless striving. But eventually he comes to believe that there is nothing
better than this enjoyment. He calls his listeners to be joyful, to experience
good, and enjoy pleasure (3:12–13).[25]

This refrain—to eat, drink, and enjoy your work—is woven throughout
the book's chapters (see 3:12–13; 5:17–19; 8:15; 9:7–9). These have a
crescendo effect in that at first the speaker is describing what he has observed
about life. In chapter 9 he makes this an imperative for the reader/listener.
Go, he says, eat, drink, enjoy.[26] He offers a radically different perspective on
the life of faith than virtually all other Old Testament authors. It is shocking
and unexpected in biblical literature. Either the author is pessimistic about
life or simply understanding that life is a striving after the wind ("Vanity,
vanity, all is vanity!" 1:2). Unlike the Song of Songs, Qolelet identifies the
pleasures of life as a gift from God. He is thinking theologically about what
has been given us; there is implied gratitude to God for life's enjoyment.
Enjoying life's pleasures is not merely tolerated, but is God approved,
perhaps even a duty to taste life's pleasures to their fullest.

> Go, eat your bread with joy and drink your wine with a glad
> heart, for God has already approved our actions. At all times let
> your clothes be white, and may oil in your head be never lacking.
> Enjoy life with a wife whom you love all the days of your fleeting
> life that God has given you under the sun—all your fleeting days.
> For that is your portion in life and in the work in which you work
> under the sun. (Eccl. 9:7–9)

A sermon series that includes some consideration of the perspective of
Qohelet raises important and interesting questions about life, the enjoyment
of the world, the call to robust living. Before we discount it and allow our
time-honored flesh/spirit dichotomies to rule and control our interpretive
response to Ecclesiastes, we should allow the presence of this book in our
canon to bring forth important questions for our living. Do we have a
theology of pleasure? Is God disappointed when we delight in the world

around us–nature, companionship, food and drink, our sexualities? Does our delight, delight God?

Reflective Questions

Our two sermon series–one on domestic abuse and one on enjoying life's pleasures, our sexualities–invite interesting questions. Are we to spend time reaching out for justice? Or are we to enjoy the world and its human pleasures? Are these exclusive of each other, or can we do both? Is Ecclesiastes 3 the answer to our dilemma? Might there be a time, a season, for everything under heaven–a time to be born, die, plant, pluck up, kill, heal, break down, build up, weep, laugh, mourn, dance, throw away stones and gather them, embrace, not embrace, seek, lose, keep, throw away, tear, sew, keep silence, speak, love, hate, a time for war and for peace? Are there times when we are called to work tirelessly to change the world and times we are called to enjoy its beauty and wonder and pleasure?

5

One Step Forward, Two Steps Back: Preaching Maturity from Proverbs

By Richard Nelson

Over the main gate of Selwyn College, Cambridge, a gold leaf Greek capitals proclaim ΣΤΗΚΕΤΕ ΕΝ ΤΗ ΠΙΣΤΕΙ ΑΝΔΡΙΖΕΣΘΕ. This is 1 Corinthians 16:13, translated by the KJV as "stand fast in the faith, quit you like men" and by the politically incorrect ESV as "stand firm in the faith, act like men." The Greek verb "act like a man" is used to denote warlike courage in the Septuagint (e.g., it is used five times in Joshua). The root behind this verb is the noun "man" used in the sense of adult male human being (*aner*, genitive *andros*). The New Testament equates maturity and manhood in three other places. Most well-known is Paul's: "When I was a child, I spoke like a child, ...; when I became an adult [literally "man"], I put an end to childish ways" (1 Cor. 13:11). The author of Ephesians urges Christians to "come to the unity of the faith and of the knowledge of the Son of God, to maturity [*eis andra teleion*, literally "to mature manhood"], to the measure of the full stature of Christ" (Eph. 4:13). Using this same language of *teleios* (mature, perfect) and *aner* (man), James states that the believer who avoids mistakes in speech is a mature or "perfect man" (Jas. 3:2, cf. RSV).

The importance of growing from childhood to maturity is a pervasive theme in scripture, particularly in the New Testament epistles (1 Cor. 3:1–2; 14:20; Gal. 4:1–3; Eph. 4:13–15; Phil. 3:15; Col. 4:12; Heb. 5:12–14; 6:1; Jas. 1:4; 1 Pet. 2:2). Colossians 1:28 specifically relates the teaching of wisdom to growth in maturity (cf. 1 Cor. 2:6).

Maturity as an Old Testament Theme

This essay investigates maturity as a homiletical theme in Proverbs. This ancient book is a collection of aphorisms and lessons originally directed to young men with the goal of helping them grow up. However, the theme of growing up first appears in the Genesis story of the garden. The first man starts out really as the first boy. His maturation begins with his earliest steps in language acquisition and vocabulary growth as he names the animals. However, it is really when God adds Woman to the scene that maturity begins to take off. In Genesis 2:23, Man moves from a state of sexual latency and ignorance to "This at last is bone of my bones and flesh of my flesh." Wow! Girls don't have cooties after all, but are something special! This starts the process of emotional distancing and detachment from parents to engagement in a central relationship of adulthood: "a man leaves his father and his mother and clings to his wife."

In Genesis 3, the first humans participate in the universal journey from childhood to maturity. They begin by living a sheltered life in a sort of kindergarten of Eden. However, there are some sharp educational edges in that garden: a delicious-looking tree, an unexplained prohibition, and Snake's thought-provoking arguments. The human couple grows from the innocuous nakedness of early childhood to mature feelings that lead to wearing aprons of fig leaves around their waists. At first they do not know good and evil–a Hebrew way of speaking about which choices are helpful and which are harmful. Not knowing good and evil is standard Old Testament language for a childlike lack of understanding (Deut. 1:39; 1 Kgs. 3:9; Isa. 7:15–16). Ironically, therefore, Woman actually does not know what she needs to know to choose wisely, but then it is precisely her bad choice (and Man's passive acquiescence) that leads to opened eyes and adult knowledge. The two grow up and must leave their sheltered nursery to encounter the cold, cruel world of adult existence: work, childbirth, patriarchy, futility, and the shadow of dusty death. Yet they have also achieved something wonderful: wisdom and maturity. The fruit of the tree, as Woman perceptively understood, was "desired to make one wise" (3:6). So they go forth from the garden and the tree of life sadder, but also wiser.[1]

The theme of maturity appears elsewhere in the Old Testament. Joseph starts off as a spoiled tattletale and self-absorbed narcissist (Gen. 37:2, 5–10), but after years of experiencing the school of hard knocks (slavery, a *femme fatale*, prison), he emerges as wise and discerning (41:39). After some judicious (and admittedly vindictive) testing of his brothers, he brings his family back together with forgiveness and perceptive wisdom (Gen. 45:5–8, 24; 50:19–21).

Solomon's dream request also explores the theme of wisdom and maturity. The NJPS captures this well: "but I am a young lad, with no experience in leadership" (1 Kgs. 3:7). So he asks for and is granted the essentials of mature wisdom: "an understanding mind" and the capacity to "discern between good and evil" (1 Kgs. 3:9, 12; cf. Gen.3:5). As Proverbs 3:13–16 teaches, riches and long life will come once wisdom is achieved (cf. 1 Kgs. 3:11, 13–14).

Solomon's son Rehoboam provides the negative paradigm of not growing up into adult responsibility (1 Kgs. 12:6–16). He refuses to pay attention to the wise advice of senior members of his father's administration and instead listens to the young hotheads. They want him to brag that he is tougher than his father ("my little one [finger, phallus?] is thicker," v. 10), but his refusal to negotiate means that he ends up with a divided kingdom and the short end of the stick. He should have learned the wisdom of Proverbs 10:14, 15:1, and 18:16. Indeed, the misfortune of having a childish ruler was proverbial (Eccl. 10:16; Isa. 3:4–5).

Then there is the book of Job. Whatever a reader may think of Job's three friends, the truly annoying character in the book is Elihu, who appears in Job 32. Elihu previews the theological position taken up by God in chapters 38–41, but he is also a brash, garrulous, egotistical youngster with little respect for his elders (32:6–10, 18–22; contrast Prov. 10:19; 16:31; 20:29).

Youth is the time for sins (Job 13:26; Ps. 25:7; Ezek. 23:19, 21); in old age one repents of them (Prov. 5:11–13). Yet youth does not necessarily mean folly or incapability. It is maturity that counts, not one's chronological age. David's youth was disparaged (1 Sam. 16:11; 17:33, 42), but proved no obstacle to being anointed as future king or overcoming Goliath. In the former case it is because Yahweh "looks on the heart" (1 Sam. 16:7). In the latter case David already has a mature level of skills and insight (1 Sam. 17:34–36, 37, 45–47). Jeremiah's claim of immaturity was overwhelmed by God's call to prophetic office (Jer. 1:6–7).

Proverbs: A Manual for Maturity

The broader meaning of the Old Testament word for wisdom (*hokmâ*) is skill, as in tailoring (Exod. 28:3), weaving (Exod. 35:26), construction (Exod. 36:1), or metalwork (1 Kgs. 7:14). Accordingly, a good definition of wisdom is "skill in living." Wisdom is a matter of know-how. A wise person knows how to live a happy, productive, and satisfying life. Wisdom is the practical ability to fit into the order of the social and physical world and master life's problems. Thus, wisdom was concerned with all areas of life, from table manners to foreign policy. Actually, "skill in living" seems to be a pretty good definition of maturity as well.

The life-setting of Proverbs is education, the process of moving children into adulthood (Prov. 22:6, 15; 29:15). Israelite wisdom functioned to bring about maturity in the young in two social locations: the urban wisdom school where young men destined for public service were trained, and the village, where traditional precepts were passed on by elders and wise women. A teacher skilled in wisdom would address his or her young charge as "son" (Prov. 3:1–2; 4:20; 5:1). The expression "my son" (NRSV "my child") occurs 23 times in Proverbs. In one section (31:1–9), the mother of Lemuel (king of Massa) gives him advice. Children are to cherish parental instruction (1:8–9; 15:5). The instruction given in 1:10–19 would certainly sound familiar to any parent or child today: don't run around with a bad crowd; don't let others influence you; crime doesn't pay.

Wise children were a great advantage to parents. They meant a secure retirement (23:22) and were a source of pride (10:1; 15:20; 23:23–25; 29:17). Properly raised children rewarded parents with diligence (10:5), wise speech (23:15–16), and righteousness (28:7). In contrast, a foolish child meant parental shame (17:21, 25; 19:26; 29:15).

From our perspective, the educational philosophy of Proverbs is a mixed bag. Start early if you want permanent results (22:6). Because the natural world was created according to wisdom principles (3:19–20), the young student of wisdom was encouraged to learn it by personal observation and comparison: "Go to the ant, you lazybones; consider its ways, and be wise" (6:6–8). Other instructive associations are put forward in 30:18–19, 21–23, 24–28, 29–31. Children just naturally do foolish things, but a good beating will set them right. Passages like 13:24, 19:19, 23:13–14, and 29:15 are still favorites with those who favor old-fashioned corporal punishment. Yet parental restraint is also advised (19:18).

The themes of Proverbs are the hallmarks of maturity: diligence and hard work (10:4; 12:27; 13:4; 20:13; 28:19 in contrast to 24:30–34), thinking before speaking (10:19; 13:3; 14:23; 18:2, 13), humility (11:2; 12:9; 16:5, 18; 21:4), and keeping one's priorities straight (11:4, 28; 15:17; 17:1; 16:19). The mature person can keep a secret (11:13; 20:19) and avoids gossip (16:28; 26:20, 22). Perhaps most difficult of all, the mature person knows how to accept criticism graciously and profit from it (9:8–9; 12:1; 15:31–32; 17:10).

Since the audience of Proverbs consisted of young men, the sexual aspect of maturity receives special attention. Prostitutes were a feature of Israelite society, and adultery was not unheard of. No doubt young men studying in urban wisdom schools, perhaps away from parental supervision, were especially vulnerable. Thus, the dangerous loose woman is the subject of four extensive poems.[2] Proverbs 2:16–19 describes the unpleasant results of involvement with her. Proverbs 5:1–23 speaks of her deceptive allure and the traps she sets for the naive. Proverbs 6:23–35 describes the lure of her beauty and the disgrace that follows adultery. As we shall see below, 7:1–27 vividly describes the seduction of an unwary young man.

Preaching Maturity—Not Only for Children

The need to grow in maturity, like all aspects of sanctification, is not restricted to any one age group. This is obvious from the frequent appearance of this theme in the New Testament epistles, which were directed to multigenerational communities of believers ("the household of faith," Gal. 6:10 RSV; cf. Titus 2). Elements of personal maturity, no matter what one's age, would certainly include:

- Take responsibility for your actions.
- Delay gratification.
- Learn from mistakes.
- Accept the reality of the way things are.
- Get over the past.
- Do your share.
- Put things in perspective.
- Make mid-course corrections.
- Balance humility with confidence, speech with silence, work with leisure, autonomy with attachment, and so on.

Making the challenge to grow up in the faith as the main thrust of a sermon will seem entirely natural to preachers of some denominations, but a dangerous flirtation with legalism and moralistic preaching to others. Christian maturity falls under the category of sanctification, a theological topic likely to generate more heat than light in ecumenical discussions. Consider John Wesley: "Who has wrote [sic] more ably than Martin Luther on justification by faith alone?

And who was more ignorant of the doctrine of sanctification, or more confused in his conceptions of it?"[3]

In some denominational traditions, the format of the didactic sermon or the tendency to advise people on how to improve their Christian lives is both acceptable and expected. In other traditions, it is considered more proper to preach the good news vigorously and then to provide a few illustrative examples of how hearers might apply the implications of that gospel to their daily lives. In what follows, I will seek to take the second path.

Interpreting Proverbs 8:1–8, 19–31

In the Revised Common Lectionary, varying verse selections from this text are appointed for the Easter Vigil (years ABC) and Trinity Sunday (year C). These choices reflect a traditional Christological interpretive direction: Christ is pre-existent Wisdom, who invites us to follow his teachings.

Wisdom's description of herself as the earliest element of God's creation, joyfully present while the rest of creation unfolds (Prov. 8:22–31), immediately attracts our attention. This is no surprise, for it provided raw material for the development of New Testament Christology (John 1:2; Col. 1:15–17; Rev. 3:14). It remains a source of inspiration for theology constructed around the topic of gender. However, the thematic center of the text is not really its description of pre-existent Wisdom, but its portrayal of Wisdom's address to the naïve and foolish—that is to say, the immature. In other words, verses 4–5 constitute the text's rhetorical focus for which the other elements of the text, including the depiction of pre-existent Wisdom, provide support. "All who live" are to heed Wisdom's call. In her ensuing speech of self-praise, she tells us why:

- Her words are worthy, straightforward, and true (vv. 6–9).
- Her results are useful and beneficial (vv. 10–21).
- She is God's first creation, present as the world was formed, delighting in humanity (vv. 22–31).

Thus, verses 22–31 describe Wisdom's significance in the heavenly world in order to confirm her value in the world of humans. Wisdom's pre-existence and cosmic significance provide support and evidence for the truth of verses 6–21, which in turn motivate those addressed to obey the imperatives of Wisdom's invitation: "learn, acquire" (v. 5), "hear" (v. 6), "take" (v. 10).

Once we understand that verses 4–5 constitute the center of the text, we can see that the whole of verses 1–32 parallels 1:20–33 in function and shape. In the first chapter of Proverbs, Wisdom's invitation grows directly out of the purpose of the book as set forth in 1:1–6. The maturity theme is especially clear in 1:4: "to teach shrewdness to the simple, knowledge and prudence to the young."

Proverbs 8:1–3 form a pleasing envelope construction: wisdom calls (v. 1) / locations (vv. 2–3) / she cries out (last word of v. 3). The negative question of verse 1 is a way of making an emphatic, positive assertion. This is not the wisdom of the ivory tower. She mixes in with the crowd of daily life in the city's streets. She cries out in the high traffic areas of crossroad and gateway. Like a teacher or prophet addressing throngs in public places, her voice is loud. She addresses all, but especially the "simple," the *peta'yim*–that is, the untaught young men who are immature and need to learn.

Verses 4–5 provide a contrasting vocabulary map for the categories of "immature" and "mature":

- "Simple ones"–*peta'yim*–designates those who need wisdom (1:22). These are the gullible and inexperienced. "Simple" is not a completely negative term like "fool," but it still represents an undesirable state of affairs that needs to be overcome by listening and learning. Young people, endangered by their immaturity, are among the simple (1:4; 7:7).
- "Fools"–*kesîlîm* (NRSV "you who lack it [intelligence])–are stock characters in Proverbs. The generic fool shows up about 50 times, sometimes as an injudicious, incompetent young person (17:21, 25; 10:1). The fool tends to be a hopeless case, resistant to learning (16:22; 17:16, 24; 18:2; 23:9).
- "Prudence"– *'ormâ*–is practical intelligence and shrewdness (in the positive sense). "Prudence" is morally neutral; Snake in Genesis

3 possesses this quality (using the adjective). A good colloquial translation would be "smarts." For examples of how the prudent act, see Proverbs 10:5, 19; 12:16, 23; 13:16; 14:15; 22:3.

• Heart—*leb*—is the site of thought, planning, and will. What NRSV translates as "acquire intelligence" is literally "instruct your heart" or "make your heart understand." The expression is similar to the "hearing heart" requested by Solomon in his prayer for maturity (1 Kgs. 3:9).

In Proverbs 8:6–8, Wisdom presents herself as reliable, trustworthy. Her words are straight and "on the level" in contrast to those of the strange woman of the previous chapters, especially chapter 7 (2:16; 5:3; 6:4; 7:21). Verse 19 measures the value of Wisdom in comparison with precious things. In verse 20, Wisdom again emphasizes that she is reliable, and in verse 21, she describes the material benefits she has to offer.

In verses 22–31, Wisdom offers her resumé, in which she emphasizes the relationship she has with the Creator and humanity. Her self-praise falls into two parts. In verses 22–26, she boasts that she was the first entity created. In verses 27–31, she reveals where she was and what she was up to when God made the rest of creation. In spite of what some have asserted about this text, Wisdom is not a co-creator with God but rather a facet of creation. "Yahweh" is in emphatic position at the start of verses 22–26 and is the subject of the verbs. Wisdom's point is that she was in a close relationship to God's acts of creation and so knows what she is talking about.

NRSV renders verse 22 as "at the beginning," but its marginal translation is equally likely, "as the beginning." In either case, Wisdom is the first entity created. Verses 24–26 employ the classic creation language of "when there was no" to indicate her absolute priority in the order of creation. This is the language of the ancient creation myths and of Gen. 2:5–"when no plant of the field...no herb of the field...God had not caused it to rain... no one to till the ground." There were no depths, springs, mountains, hills, or soil on the earth's surface. The language used for Wisdom's origin envisions a birthing process: "I was brought forth...I was brought forth" (Prov. 8:24–25)–that is to say, I was birthed. The passive verb indicates divine action. In addition, the verb translated by the NRSV in verse 22 as "created" (*qananî*) more generally means "acquired," and here it probably refers to divine begetting or procreation (as suggested by Gen. 4:1). The NAB follows this interpretation boldly, translating "The LORD begot me, the first-born of his ways," and the ESV margin takes the same direction with "fathered me." This radical image sets Wisdom apart as a unique creation in contrast to the more pedestrian construction language used for the other elements of creation in verses 26–29: "shaped," "made," "established," "drew a circle" (the horizon or the edge of the disk of dry land), "made firm," "established" ("fixed securely"), "assigned," and "marked out."

Verses 27–31 describe what Wisdom did while Yahweh was creating. Six creative actions are introduced in turn with "when" (better, "while"). In the first of these phrases, Wisdom boasts, "I was there" (v. 27a). Following the other phrases, she says four things about herself:

- She was "beside" Yahweh.
- She was an *'amôn*. This puzzling word is usually taken to be "master worker" (NRSV), "faithful one" (NJPS "confidant"), or "darling child" (compare REB). It is best understood in light of the Mesopotamian ancient sage who mediated knowledge from the heavenly world.[4]
- She was a delight every day ("*his* delight" is an NRSV interpretive translation).
- She rejoiced before Yahweh, in the "inhabited world," and in human beings. Note the concentric pattern in verses 30–31: delight / rejoicing // rejoicing / delighting.

It is this last self-assertion that is most important for the rhetoric of the unit. It takes us back to verses 4–5 and motivates the simple to listen. Not only are Wisdom's words straight and advantageous (vv. 6–8, 19–21), not only do her primeval origins endow her words with authority, but she has a gracious, cordial attitude toward the human race. She can be trusted to want the best for us. Both ancient and modern theologians have read into this text the notion that Wisdom here is the personification of a divine attribute or a co-worker and partner in creation. Neither is true in this particular text. Wisdom here is the poetic personification of an abstract concept and, though she is present at creation and rejoices in it, she does not do any creating herself. The fundamental point is that she addresses us and delights in us.

Preaching Proverbs 8:1–8, 19–31

The text seeks to persuade its simple-minded, inexperienced audience to learn maturity and wisdom. This persuasion is based on Wisdom's own self-recommendation. One could rewrite this in the language of advertising copy:

- You can trust us to stand behind our widget.
- Our widget is better/tastier/more effective than the inferior widgets offered by our competitors.
- In the long run, it will pay off for you to acquire a superior quality widget.
- We have been in the widget business for a long time. In fact, we invented them.

One way to avoid legalistic or moralistic preaching is to construct a "text sentence" with God or God's agent as the grammatical subject, and then derive a "sermon sentence" from it. A possible text sentence on Proverbs

8 could be "Wisdom invites the simple to learn prudence, with words that are straightforward, rewarding, and authoritative." An evangelical (that is, gospel-driven) sermon that follows the text's focus on verses 4–5 and takes the maturity theme seriously could grow out of this sermon sentence: "God's Word invites those who are immature in faith and teaches them mature prudence and good judgment." In designing a sermon flowing from this sentence, the preacher might want to draw attention to these items drawn from a canonical reading of the text:

- Both inside and outside the community of faith, there are many who are immature in faith and conduct, thinking and acting in naïve ways.
- God's word is a public word and an assertive word. It speaks to all with a clear message and seeks urgently to convince all to listen and be transformed.
- God's word is honest, forthright, and straightforward. It does not engage in manipulation or trickery.
- God's word is profitable to all who take its instruction to heart. When read or preached, it is a means of grace leading us to faith in God.
- Jesus Christ is God's Word in the most fundamental sense, "eternally begotten...not made,...through him all things were made" (John 1 and the Nicene Creed).

A Sermon Series on Maturity

Four texts not used by the Revised Common Lectionary reflect the theme and vocabulary of maturity.[5]

Prov. 1:8–19—Steer Clear of Criminal Gangs

This text is structured by a threefold repetition of the address "my child" (vv. 8, 10, 15), the last two followed by prohibitions "do not consent" and "do not walk." The "my child" address is a sign that growth in maturity in the theme (compare other texts in this proposed series: 19:27; 23:15, 19). It is easy to imagine a contemporary setting for these verses. Dad sits Junior down and says, "Look, your mother and I want to talk to you. We don't like the crowd of thugs you've been hanging around with lately. Bad company can get you into big trouble." Dad speaks; Mom remains in the supportive background. Father speaks "instructions" (*mûsar*, elsewhere "discipline"; see below under 19:20–27) and Mother *tôrâ* ("teaching"). This imagined setting takes on added poignancy if we picture it taking place in a neighborhood infested with gangs luring impressionable youths into membership.

What is to be avoided is described as a plot to mug people and enjoy ill-gotten gains. The situation is extreme, but as a theatrical "worst-case scenario," it has pedagogical value. It is something like those videos of drunk driving accidents shown to high school students. Negative rhetoric describes the criminals. They fall into the category of sinners (13:21; 23:17). In verse 15, a balanced parallelism reverses negative into positive ("do not walk... keep your foot from"). This parallelism underscores what is unacceptable, and when taken with verse 16, makes a pleasing concentric pattern (walk / foot // feet / hurry). "Entice" characterizes their blandishments. This verb denotes "manipulate someone into an action harmful to him- or herself." It is the verbal root behind the "simple" person who plays such an important role in the maturity theme (7:7; 8:5). The verb sometimes edges over into "seduce," and Delilah's manipulation of Samson is the perfect narrative example (Judg. 14:15; 16:5). Of course, it is the naïve, inexperienced youngster who is most easily taken advantage of. The villains "are greedy" for "gain." Both verb and noun are from a root one could translate "take one's cut." The words signify unjust, illegitimate profit (Prov. 15:27; 28:16). The criminals' invitation "come with us" and "lie in wait" are paralleled in the adulterous woman text considered below (7:12, 18).

A rhetoric of dramatic quotation (also used in 7:14–20) simultaneously depicts and undermines the enticing argument of the criminals. They motivate the targeted youth with a promise of lots of loot, a congenial life together as partners in crime, and an egalitarian division of proceeds. But the father who quotes them works in his own negative evaluation in verse 11: "wantonly" (that is, without cause) and "innocent." They are made to brag that they are like the aggressive realm of the dead that gulps people down whole.

The text supports its teaching with four motivational arguments:

- The respect and honor a son or daughter owes to parents (v. 8).
- The image of parental instruction as publically visible ornaments, intended to counter the booty promised by the criminals (v. 9; 4:9).
- The poorly understood proverb in verse 17. As a warning for the immature addressee, this seems to say that even dumb birds know enough not to fly into a net they have seen baited. Or does it refer to the scoundrels who aren't even as smart as birds?
- Crimes rebound back on those who commit them (vv. 18–19).

Biblical scholars often term this last notion the doctrine of retribution, but the less negative phrase "act-consequence relationship" is preferable. A classic statement of this principle, almost viewed as a natural law in wisdom literature, is 5:21–23. Proverbs 1:18 picks up vocabulary from what the criminals have said in verse 11 ("lie in wait," "ambush") and uses it to set a fitting and deadly retribution upon them. The act-consequence relationship continues in verse 19: the end result of greed for unjust gain is the death of those who come to possess it.

If one is preaching this text in an urban setting, with gang graffiti scrawled on the church walls, to parents frantic about the attractions of gang life, the move from text to sermon probably is automatic. However, there are other tempting crimes and conspiracies that do not involve violent attacks on our neighbors. Rural America is infested with meth labs. Business leaders go to jail. "Costly things," "booty," and "purse" are enticing to all of us, and those with immature consciences or value systems are particularly vulnerable.

To craft a gospel-oriented sermon on this text, one could contrast the deadly consequences (vv. 18–19) of the criminals' invitation to "come" with the counter-invitation offered by Wisdom (9:5) and Jesus (Matt. 11:28). The invitation to crime leads to death; the invitation of Jesus leads to life. A sermon sentence could be "In the context of alluring temptations to seek wealth in corrupt ways that lead to death, Jesus invites us to come to him, acquire genuine treasure, and live." Another approach would be to focus on the parallel, God-given vocations of parenting (to teach maturity) and children (to learn maturity and "just say no").

Prov. 7:6–23–Watch Out for Sexual Temptation

The topic of sexual transgression may be considered inappropriate by some preachers and many congregations. I am sure, however, that John Holbert, in whose honor this volume has been produced, would not hesitate a moment to treat this as an appropriate and needed topic.

Again, we are in the realm of danger to the immature, as indicated by the preceding "my child, listen" in Prov. 7:1. Here is our youthful male–"simple one" again–out for a perilous nocturnal adventure, thoughtlessly going "like an ox to the slaughter" (v. 22). The scene is set as the speaker, perhaps Wisdom herself or some other woman, gazes out her widow lattice. This is something women do often in the Bible (Judg. 5:20; 2 Sam. 6:16; 2 Kgs. 9:30). The speaker observes an unfolding seduction. The scene is similar to what the woman figure of Folly does in 9:13–18. Negative rhetoric is piled up against the woman. Disguised as a prostitute, she turns out to be something worse, a faithless wife (v. 10). Her heart is cunning with hidden intent (v. 10). Out on the street by "her corner" (v. 8), she is the complete opposite of the stay-at-home wife doubtlessly valued by the text's original audience (v. 11). Like the thugs in the previous text, she lies in wait (v. 12). She reverses expected social norms by being the aggressor (contrast the use of "seize" in Deut. 22:25, 28) and shows an insolent, impudent expression (v. 13; cf. 21:29). She kisses him publicly (cf. Song 8:1).

Again, as was the case with the robber gang in chapter 1, a tempting quotation is put into her mouth. Her rhetoric appeals to the senses and appetites. Her sacrifice means she has meat to put on the table. But this holy meat is to be eaten in a context of impurity! She has come out to seek love (compare the night quest in Song 3:1–4). Verses 16–17 describe her preparations. Her bed is draped in colorful imported fabrics and perfumed with the romantic fragrances of Song 4:14. "Let's drink our fill of sex…taste together the pleasure of love" captures the steamy rhetoric of verse 18 better than the colorless NRSV. She concludes by arguing it will be perfectly safe (vv. 19–20). Her husband has taken a lot of money to cover his expenses. It is dark now (v. 9), and he isn't due home until the bright full moon. Verse 21 closes the quoted speech and provides a negative evaluation.

The seduction succeeds as the simple fellow suddenly (or "thoughtlessly") follows her (vv. 22–23). The images of slaughter and trap involve a bit of sexual double meaning: His own innards are penetrated; he enters a snare. Typical of the simple, he does not know that his actions endanger his very life (cf. 4:19; 9:18; 28:22).

There are several hazards in preaching this text, most obviously its "blame the woman" perspective. One way to finesse this would be to emphasize the theme of betrayal over that of sexual allure. She has betrayed her relationship to God (v.14; "sacrifice," "my vows") and her husband (v. 20) and converted them both into rhetorical ammunition. Moreover, the young simpleton has betrayed his own best interests, and in the context of Proverbs at least, his parents (17:25; 29:3).

To avoid preaching a moralistic sermon, the preacher could take the direction suggested for the previous text and contrast the life-giving invitation of the gospel to the seductive allure of various sorts of infidelity. Contextually, this woman's words set up a contrast to Wisdom's invitations in chapters 8 and 9. Both address the simple (7:7; 8:5; 9:4, 16). This woman approaches in darkness (7:9), but Wisdom speaks in public (8:2–3; cf. 9:3). This woman's motives and tactics contrast with those of Wisdom (7:10–12; 8:8, 20). Her lips are smooth (7:21 literally; NRSV "seductive speech"), but right things come from the lips of Wisdom that reject wickedness (8:6–7). This woman prepares her bed for illicit sex (7:16–17); Wisdom prepares a banquet table (9:2). The house of this woman is a dangerous location (7:8, 27); Wisdom's seven-pillared house is a place of insight (9:1, 6). Her words lead to death (7:22–23); listening to Wisdom leads to life (8:35).

Prov. 19:20–27–Listen to Advice

Here the expression "my child," marking this as a maturity text, comes at the end in verse 27. Individual proverbs on various topics have been gathered together and bookended by the word "instruction" (*mûsar*) in verses 20 and 27. Thus verses 21–26 constitute the "instruction" promoted by verses 20 and 27. Verses 20, 25, and 27 are about acquiring wisdom. Verses 21 and 23 explore the vital role of a proper understanding of Yahweh. The other verses advocate wise virtues: loyalty and honesty (v. 22), diligence (v. 24), and honoring parents (v. 26).

"Instruction" (*mûsar*) appears at the beginning and the end of the text. This word is significant for the maturity theme and found in two other texts in this series (1:8; 23:23). It derives from the verbal root *yasar*, "educate/discipline in order to shape conduct," often used in the context of childrearing (Deut. 8:5; 21:18; Prov. 19:18; 29:17; 31:1). The noun *mûsar* can refer to a body of knowledge to be transmitted (1:8; 19:20, 27; 23:23; by a parent in 4:1; 8:33; 13:1; 15:5). When translated "discipline," the word indicates corporal punishment to encourage learning (3:11–12; 13:29; 23:13).

The audience is to listen to and internalize *mûsar*. Its educational goals are oriented toward the "end" (Prov. 19:20; NRSV "future"). Proverbs 14:12 and 16:25 speak of the "end" as death. In Proverbs 19:20, however, "end" also implies life in the sense of a full, satisfying existence stretching into peaceful old age, the sort of life wisdom makes possible (3:16; 4:10). However, wisdom also means taking into account the limits placed on our plans by God's sovereignty (Prov. 19:21; cf. 16:1, 9). A person's true worth is measured by loyalty (*hesed*; fidelity to a relationship) and honesty, not riches (Prov. 19:22). Faithful obedience (that is, fear of God) is the true basis for security and a fortunate life (v. 23).

Verse 24 comically describes the lazybones (traditionally "sluggard") who appears 14 times in Proverbs. For other images of laziness, see 10:26, 22:13–16, and 24:30–34. Parents will no doubt be reminded of adolescent sleep patterns!

Proverbs 19:25 is paralleled in 21:11. There are three stock characters here. The scoffer is someone who brags about self and derides others (21:24). This sort of person is a hopeless case (9:7–8; 14:6). The immature simple one is least capable of learning when observing a scoffer being punished. So punishment, even if the scoffer learns nothing from it, can have a positive pedagogical value for others. The intelligent one, however, has matured into a superior learner—one who accepts criticism and benefits from it. Proverbs insists that to "reprove" or rebuke" (NRSV translates the same word two ways) benefits the mature (17:10; 27:5; 28:23), but does not work on the immature (9:8; 13:1). The proper task of the simple is to learn prudence (1:4; 8:5).

Proverbs 19:26 does not describe a theoretical situation. Such violence would be a temptation for adult children living in a multigenerational family and restive under the financial and social authority of elderly parents. This is the reason for the death sentence law of Exodus 21:15 and the extended diatribe of Proverbs 30:11–16. One's respect for parents and the serious effect immature behavior has on them are used as motivational factors in 10:1, 17:25, 20:20, 30:11, 17, and 23:22–25, discussed below.

Proverbs 19:27 is a tongue-in-cheek rhetorical command and requires an interpretive translation. The Hebrew says literally "Cease, my son, to hear instruction, so that you may stray from the words of knowledge." Of course, this is ironic and really means that to quit learning would be a really bad idea. The NIV captures this with "Stop listening to instruction, my son, and you will stray from the words of knowledge."

A text framed by imperatives ("listen," "accept" v. 20; "cease" v. 27) must be put into a gospel context to avoid moralistic scolding. The preacher should note how thoroughly a relationship to God permeates this text. It is good news that Yahweh controls our future, whatever our own (perhaps problematic) plans may be (v. 21). In the last analysis, it is our fear of Yahweh (obedient faith and faithful obedience) that leads to life and security. The motivations to take good advice are good ones and could be expanded by the preacher to include such motivations as a good future (v. 20), safety and security (v. 23), knowledge (vv. 25, 27), and a healthy relationship to one's parents (v. 26). The text has echoes in the teaching of Jesus that can be exploited to good advantage. The topic of an uncertain future in verse 20 may be illustrated by the story of the rich man and Lazarus (Luke 16:19–31). The parable of the rich fool (Luke 12:13–21) relates to the sentiment about human plans expressed by verse 21. Verse 23, speaking of the security that is the result of faith, suggests the Sermon on Mount (Matt. 5:6 6:25–34). Jesus' story of the son who says yes but does not actually obey (Matt. 21:28–31) could illustrate verse 26.

Prov. 23:15–25–Listen to Mom and Dad

This text is part of a self-contained unit (22:17–24:22) derived from or related to an Egyptian source, the *Instruction of Amenemope*. Wisdom was an international phenomenon (1 Kgs. 4:30). In the Egyptian text, a government official gives advice to his son. In our text, the parental education theme is clearly present in the address "my child" (Prov. 19:15, 19) and the call to "hear" and "listen" (vv. 19, 22). Motivation in verses 15–16 and 24–25 surrounds five individual instructions, forming a concentric structure.

In verses 15–16 and 24–25, personal relationship motivates the hearer. The parental teacher seeks to inspire the child by pointing out the positive effects of successful learning. The parent will rejoice in a wise offspring. Verses 15–16 have a chiastic structure: your heart / my heart // my soul / your lips. The corresponding verses 24–25 say the same thing, although the verb for "rejoice" is different from the one used in verse 15. These last verses also form a chiasm: rejoice / be glad // be glad / rejoice, and involve parallelism that includes both parents: he who begets // she who bore.

The five instructions involve prohibitions (vv. 17, 20, 22b) and admonitions to hear, listen, and buy (vv. 19, 22, 23). The parallelisms in verses 17, 18, 22, and 23 balance positive and negative statements. Two of the instructions have motivation clauses (vv. 17–18, 20–21).

- Verses 17–18 form the first instruction. Parents are concerned about those whom young people regard as heroes. Some fall into the category of "sinners." This warning is motivated by a call to consider the long-term goal of a future ("end"; cf. 19:20) involving a life of well-being and honor, not one marred by tragedy or cut off in its prime.

- Verse 19 uses the common metaphor of "way," signifying conduct. The notion of "way" is also present in 1:15, 19 and 7:25, 27. Proverbs 4:14–19 and Psalm 1 contrast the ways of the wicked and righteous.
- Verses 20–21 criticize overindulgence in meat and alcohol. The "glutton and drunkard" is a classic paradigm of irredeemable youth in Deuteronomy 21:20, where fathers and mothers are shamed by such behavior and take drastic action. Of course Jesus was accused of this very same thing (Matt. 11:19). Overeaters are the topic of Proverbs 28:7 and drunkards appear in 26:9–10. The negative effects of wine are expanded in the vignette of 23:29–35, but a reverse opinion is stated in 31:7. The motivation offered in verse 21 indicates that poverty is the expected result of excess (cf. 21:17). Too much food and drink leads to snoozing, which in turn leads to destitution. Wisdom literature affirms the principle that hard work leads to financial success (10:4; 12:27; 13:4; 20:13; 28:19). Nevertheless, wealth does not matter in the really important aspects of life (11:14, 28; 15:17; 17:1). In God's eyes, rich and poor are equal (22:2), and the poor are to be respected (17:5; 22:16, 22–23).
- Proverbs 19:22 instructs the hearer to defer to father and mother. This theme reappears as a motivation in verses 24–25.
- Verse 23 uses the metaphor of purchase to urge acquiring and holding on to what is most valuable (cf. Isa. 55:1). It sums up a mature person's priorities: truth, wisdom, instruction (*mûsar*), and understanding.

In preaching this text, one will want to begin with and constantly refer to the relational framework set up by verses 15–16 and 24–25. In the arena of faith, one's childlike relationship to a parental God motivates attempts to become mature. As children we can make God glad ("there is more joy in heaven," Luke 15:7) by growing in maturity. The relationship between human parenting and obedience to God is explored in Matthew 12:48–50 and Luke 11:27–28 (and is taken in different directions by Rom. 8:14–17 and Col. 3:20). In the light of the gospel, Proverbs 23:18–"Surely there is a future, and your hope will not be cut off"–sounds a word of grace. This theme of future hope can be explored with the help of Romans 5:2–5 and 8:24–25. The parables of treasure found in a field and the valuable pearl (Matt. 13:44, 46) illustrate the advice to buy what is truly valuable (Prov. 23:23), and the urging not to sell it is echoed in Matthew 16:23. Careful speech and the avoidance of drunkenness and gluttony (Prov. 23:16, 20–21) are standard elements of New Testament parenesis (1 Cor. 6:10; Eph. 5:18; 1 Pet. 4:3). Luke 21:34 offers the best reason imaginable not to overindulge.

A gospel-oriented sermon could emphasize that God makes us God's children and gives us the hope of a wonderful future. We can make God glad by believing ("buy truth") and obeying ("fear")—for example, by avoiding envy and overindulgence, watching our conduct, and honoring parents.

6

Body/Parts:
Body Image in the Old Testament

Roy L. Heller

John Holbert is a master of homiletics. But, as with any remarkable preacher, John is also a remarkable reader of biblical texts. He has a way of taking what is seemingly simple and straightforward and showing the complexity, depth, beauty, irony, and surprises that lie–or, perhaps, lurk– right under the surface. The following article is offered to John in honor and in affection for all he has taught me as a colleague and meant to me as a friend.

Ever since my children were old enough to go to Sunday school, the liturgy of the car ride home from church has always been the same. We get in the car. I pull out of the parking lot and onto the street. I look in the rearview mirror and see them in the backseat. Then I ask the question, "What did you learn in Sunday school today?" After their (usually) one sentence answer, we have a discussion about whatever subject they might have talked about that morning.

One on occasion, when my son Noah was about six or seven, I asked him my usual question, to which he responded, "When God made the world." I gushed. I asked which story (Gen. 1 or 2) they talked about. When my son looked at me quizzically, I asked further whether the story was about God making things on different days or whether it was about God making a person out of dirt. "Different days," he answered. After blathering a two-minute mini-lecture on Genesis 1:1–2:4a–the poetic logic of the order of the things created, and the correspondence of the six days in a pattern of two groups of three–my son asked a simple question: "Abba, why aren't there any dinosaurs in the story?" I felt my brain split in two.

Initially, I wanted to tell him: "Asking questions about dinosaurs missed the point of the story as a whole. The beauty of the story was found in its message that all creation–from supernovae to electrons, from asparagus to crabgrass, from fruit flies to blue whales–was very good. Every part of creation had a place in the whole. There was nothing outside of God's care and love, and God was the source of it all. Creation was beautiful and, therefore, it was good." On the other hand, I decided to just tell him the plain truth: "The people who wrote the story didn't know that there had been dinosaurs. Because they didn't know about them, they didn't worry about putting them in the story." Ancient authors did not know about things that we know about. Because they had no direct contact with items like dinosaurs or quarks or radiators, there is no word for such things in their language, or seemingly, in their worldview.

But this also applies to things that they undoubtedly *did* have contact with but saw very differently than we do. For example, in the entire corpus of Assyrian and Babylonian writings–literally millions of words–the word for "yellow" never occurs in Akkadian. The closest corresponding word is "green"/(*warqu*) [SIG 7, IGI-gunû].[1] Even though yellow items were as ubiquitous in Mesopotamia as in Minneapolis, its citizens had no specific word to describe a "yellow" object as opposed to a "green" object. Yellow, for them, was a pale shade of green, similar to our own perception of "robin's-egg blue" and "navy blue" as being, not two different colors, but only a darker and lighter shade of the same color. If ancient Babylonians were to see a daffodil, they would not see the stem and the flower as being of two different colors, but rather a dark "*warqu*" stem topped by a light "*warqu*" flower.[2]

Human Body in the Old Testament?

When one looks at a seemingly simple and straightforward subject such as "the understanding of the human body in the Hebrew Bible," one is immediately struck by an indisputable fact: there is no word for "human body" in the Hebrew of the Old Testament. While other fields and disciplines have exploded with studies and articles on the place of "the body," or "embodiment," the field of Hebrew Bible has been relatively quiet on this front, and for good reason. It is difficult writing about something that never occurs.

The absence of a word for "human body" in the Old Testament, and conversely the centrality of the concept of human body for the New Testament, is illustrated by the articles for "Body" in two recent Bible dictionaries. In the *Anchor Bible Dictionary*, the article is divided into three primary sections: "OT and Judaism," "Greek/Hellenistic World," and "The

NT," along with a conclusion. While the entry on the understanding of the body in the Greek/Hellenistic world is a column in length and the New Testament entry is almost ten columns in length, the entry for "OT and Judaism" is only half a column in length and a quarter of it is primarily about late Aramaic and rabbinic understandings.[3] While the *New Interpreter's Dictionary of the Bible* is more equitable with the space given to the discussion of the subject between the testaments, the single-column discussion "Body in the OT" is a third the size of the discussion of "Body in the NT," in spite of the fact of the much longer and more complex corpus of materials found in the Old Testament.[4] When there is no data to work with, any report is necessarily short.

What both entries share—besides their relative brevity—is a discussion of the point that no Hebrew word in the biblical texts exactly conforms to what English calls a human body.[5] Clearly, English Bibles have the word "body" in Old Testament texts and, it seems, have had it from the earliest translations.[6] The Hebrew words that lie behind these translational (non) equivalents are, with little exception, two: hywg/*geviyyah* and rfb/*basar*.

The word *geviyyah* appears 13 times in 11 verses.[7] Although it is often translated into English as "body" in the NRSV, it also appears as "carcass" (Judg. 14:8, 9), "corpses" (Ps. 110:6) or specifically "dead bodies" (Nah. 3:3). In this same vein, even when it is translated simply as "body," it consistently refers to literal corpses (those of Saul and his sons, 1 Sam. 31:10–12) or metaphorically to a state of oppression that consigns living people to the status of being essentially "dead on their feet" (Gen.47:8; Neh. 9:37).[8] While it may be true that a "corpse" is in fact a "human body," the two terms are not equivalent or, on a certain level, even close. The image and idea and concept of the "embodiedness" of human *existence* is not the same as a "corpse," almost by definition.

The other Hebrew word that is often translated as "body," *basar*, is more common, appearing almost 300 times in over 250 verses in the Bible. In these cases, overwhelmingly in most contexts, *basar* refers, not to a general human body, but rather to literal flesh or meat, either of animals or of humans, and is usually translated as such in the NRSV. As with *geviyyah*, *basar* also clearly connotes the idea of a "corpse" or a "death-tending" person either literally or metaphorically in other passages. Outside of the legal corpora of Leviticus and Numbers, even in those cases where the NRSV translates *basar* as "body," it always refers to a literal or metaphorical corpse where the theme of death is in the immediate context (Ps. 109:24; Prov. 5:11; Eccl. 2:3; 11:10; Isa. 10:18; Ezek. 36:26).

Leviticus requires a short comment here. *Basar* is assumed to be used in two different ways in Leviticus. Often, *basar* refers to the "meat" of the sacrifices or with making gashes in the "flesh" of humans. In these cases, of course, the referent is the muscles of the animal or human instead of the idea of the whole physical individual. On the other hand, the NRSV translates *basar* as "body" in Leviticus 26 times, more than in any other book and, unlike *geviyyah* in other biblical books, in these verses it does not seem to connote a corpse or corpse-like state of human existence. The *basar* of the human in these cases is often "washed" or "bathed," and it can touch linen garments (6:10; 16:4). Furthermore, it is closely associated with "skin"/`or and, when the skin is broken or compromised through disease, the living or raw *basar* can be seen. In every one of these cases, however, it is clear that although the *basar* is washed or seen, this does not refer to the "complete physical form of a person or animal; the assemblage of parts, organs, and tissues that constitutes the whole material organism," but rather is identical with the idea of the meat/flesh concept that is used in reference to the sacrifices and the musculature in the prohibitions against gashing. The focus throughout Leviticus is on keeping those things "inside of the skin from coming "outside," and, if it does, then it must be examined and, if considered safe, the *basar* must be washed. In each of these cases, no concept of a whole body ever occurs.

How interesting it is that there does not seem to be a word that exactly, or even closely, corresponds to what we mean when we use the word "body" or "human body" in the Old Testament. Now, of course, the ancient Hebrews did not think of themselves as bodiless or disembodied. They clearly understood that people had muscles, bones, eyes, ears, throats, hands, hair, skin, and feet (both literally and, in the case of men, euphemistically). Moreover, they also knew that people had certain parts that were not commonly in view, such as the heart, liver, kidneys, intestines, and in the case of women, a womb. In other words, people clearly had parts.

The clearest examples in the Bible of this listing of a person's parts occur in the praises of the beauty of the female character and the male character in the Song of Songs. Three times in the poem, the male character lists the various parts of the female character and, using metaphors, acclaims the beauty of each one. In the first of these cases, he starts at her head and works his way down, ending at her "mountain of myrrh and the hill of frankincense" (Song 4:1–6).[9] In the second case, he concentrates on her head (6:5–7), listing her hair, teeth, and cheeks. In the third case, he begins at her feet and works his way up:

> How graceful are your feet in sandals, O queenly maiden!
> Your rounded thighs are like jewels, the work of a master hand.
> Your navel is a rounded bowl that never lacks mixed wine.
> Your belly is a heap of wheat, encircled with lilies.
> Your two breasts are like two fawns, twins of a gazelle.
> Your neck is like an ivory tower.
> Your eyes are pools in Heshbon, by the gate of Bath-rabbim.

Your nose is like a tower of Lebanon, overlooking Damascus.
Your head crowns you like Carmel, and your flowing locks are
    like purple; a king is held captive in the tresses.
How fair and pleasant you are, O loved one, delectable maiden!
(Song 7:1–6)

Not to be outdone, the female character returns the favor and lists the parts of the man as well, beginning at his head and travelling down. In her case, however, she praises him to her friends, the "daughters of Jerusalem," and not directly to the man himself:

My beloved is all radiant and ruddy, distinguished among ten
    thousand.
His head is the finest gold.
His locks are wavy, black as a raven.
His eyes are like doves beside springs of water, bathed in milk,
    fitly set.
His cheeks are like beds of spices, yielding fragrance.
His lips are lilies, distilling liquid myrrh.
His arms are rounded gold, set with jewels.
His body [more correctly, "torso"] is ivory work, encrusted with
    sapphires.
His legs are alabaster columns, set upon bases of gold.
His appearance is like Lebanon, choice as the cedars.[10]
His speech is most sweet, and he is altogether desirable.
This is my beloved and this is my friend, O daughters of
Jerusalem. (Song 5:10–16)

In all of these passages, and in the Hebrew Bible as a whole, it is clear that the writers of the various texts understood that people were composed of and had various parts.

However, it is not at all clear that they understood that those various parts were integrally connected to form a person that consisted of a "complete physical form ..., the assemblage of parts, organs, and tissues that constitutes the whole material organism."[11] It is generally assumed that the Old Testament as a whole does not understand embodied human existence in the same dichotomous way that many New Testament texts do. Throughout the corpus of Hebrew biblical texts—whether earlier or later, whether narrative, poetry, or legal material—humans are never understood as being a "spirit/soul" that inhabits a "body."

Instead, the conventional scholarly wisdom asserts that the Old Testament as a whole views human existence holistically: "What man is can only be understood in a wholistic way. Man does not possess a soul and a body, rather he is both soul and flesh, full of life and potential activity."[12] Joel Green describes it in a slightly different way: "More generally, *body* refers to the form of the human being in his or her entirety. The dualism of body and soul, familiar in certain Greek circles, has little basis in the OT, where people are souls (rather than have them) and are bodies (rather than possess them)."[13] Most scholars understand the perspective of the Old Testament in this way. Humans do not have bodies; they *are* bodies; they are the essence of embodied life; they *are* bodies, energized and animated with the "breath of life."

From the time of the Enlightenment, the West has seen things another way. With Rene Descartes' statement of his famous dictum, "Cogito ergo sum"/"I think, therefore, I am," the fact that the thinking subject is, in fact, the real person has so foundationally influenced our thinking that it has been difficult to see things differently. People are no longer thought of as their bodies (as whole entities) and not even the integral combination of their thinking selves plus their bodies. No, as an inheritance of the Enlightenment, the West has consistently seen the thinking subject as the "true person." If, however, the true self is simply a thinking subject, then this makes the "body" an absolute necessity! The thinking subject cannot access the real world except through a body. The body holds the various senses, or gateways, by which the true self encounters and knows about the physical world. This way of seeing the nature of what it means to be human is so deeply engrained, apparently, that we cannot even imagine how to describe a "human being"–even as it is understood in the Old Testament–without a reference to the "body." Therefore, when describing the Old Testament's views on what it means to be human, almost all commentators will first contrast it to the Hellenistic view (a soul trapped within a physical body). They will then, as the examples above highlight, argue that the Old Testament sees human existence holistically, as a soul (i.e., Descartes' "thinking subject") and a body together, equally important.

If, however, this is true, then we might expect to see more–or even some–or even one instance of a–statement that human bodies exist. This, in fact, never occurs in the Old Testament. People have hands, eyes, hair, teeth, "flesh," and "guts." But when those parts are considered, they are almost always considered separately, and when they are considered together, that composite whole is never called a "human body."

As we have seen, such an idea is not present in any of the contexts that *geviyyah* is used. Even though *basar* is used more frequently and in varied contexts, it almost always refers to the "flesh" that is present immediately under the skin of animals and humans, and, from that denotation, it often has the connotation of something that decays and rots, and has the trace of death associated with it. Both *geviyyah* and *basar* in the Hebrew Bible have negative connotations. The idea of "body" does not. If, in fact, humans are bodies, then why does a word for it, or even an understanding of it, never appear? It appears as if "human body," like "dinosaur," might be something that the ancient Hebrew authors never knew existed. How could this be?

Furthermore, if in fact no "body" appears in the Old Testament, how did those authors and communities view human existence?

I suspect that the answer lies in an understanding of human existence that is so closely tied with all other physical reality that designating and separating *my* physical existence as a whole (my "body") from "other" physical existence as a whole is meaningless. In other words, according to the Old Testament, not only do I not have a body, I am not a body. I am a person (*nefesh*), but my totality is never described in physical terms. In the non-Western, non-Hellenistic world of the Old Testament, there is no physical "me" that stands over and against all the physical phenomena of the world. Yes, of course, I can think and love and hope and desire. And, yes, I have hands, eyes, teeth, legs, skin, and flesh. But in the continuum between my "parts" and the rest of reality, the line that separates me from everything else is blurry.

According to the worldview of the Hebrew Bible, because I am a physical presence—but without a "body," without a clear bifurcating line between me and all else—my human existence is always and everywhere interdependent upon the rest of the physical world and both are, continually, dependent upon the God who is the source of all. I am not over and against reality; I am completely a part of reality. It is almost as if I am, through and through, the same thing as the ground upon which I walk, the land that I farm, the dust that blows in the wind (Gen. 2:7).

So far, I have discussed the concept of being human and "bodied" from a broad, top-down perspective. The topic can also be considered from particular texts themselves, from a specific, bottom-up perspective. Let us look at a few texts that have this topic at their center.

Psalm 32: How Our Emotions Affect Us

Introduction
> [1] Happy are those whose transgression is forgiven,
>> whose sin is covered.
> [2] Happy are those to whom the LORD imputes no iniquity,
>> and in whose spirit there is no deceit.

Confession Is Good: A Personal Witness
> [3] While I kept silence, my body wasted away[14]
>> through my groaning all day long.
> [4] For day and night your hand was heavy upon me;
>> my strength was dried up as by the heat of summer.[15]
> [5] Then I acknowledged my sin to you,
>> and I did not hide my iniquity;
> I said, "I will confess my transgressions to the LORD,"
>> and you forgave the guilt of my sin.

Prayer and Protection

⁶ Therefore let all who are faithful offer prayer to you;[16]
> at a time of distress, the rush of mighty waters shall not reach
> them.
⁷ You are a hiding place for me;
> you preserve me from trouble;
> you surround me with
> glad cries of deliverance.

A "Bit" of Wisdom

⁸ I will instruct you and teach you the way you should go; I will
> counsel you with my eye upon you. ⁹ Do not be like a horse or
> a mule, without understanding, whose temper must be curbed
> with bit and bridle, else it will not stay near you.

Conclusion

¹⁰ Many are the torments of the wicked,
> but steadfast love surrounds those who trust in the Lord.
¹¹ Be glad in the Lord and rejoice, O righteous,
> and shout for joy, all you upright in heart.

Psalm 32 is an unusual psalm that provides a personal witness of
the effects that stubbornness and self-deceit can have upon those who
harbor those attitudes as well as the remarkable healing that results from
an acknowledgment of one's own wrongdoing. The psalm as a whole is
divided into five stanzas. The flow of the psalm through the stanzas has
a kind of narrative logic that drives the psalm forward and, finally, ties it
together into a whole.

The first stanza introduces the basic message and meaning of the psalm:
people who have a clear and open relationship between themselves and
God, with none of the interfering clutter of sin or iniquity or deceit, are
blessed or fortunate or "happy." Even within this stanza, however, there is
a delicate logic and flow. In verse 1, the nouns "transgression" and "sin" are
accompanied by passive participial verbs, "is forgiven" and "is covered."
The discussion of sin and forgiveness begins in a very static and passive way.
People are fortunate if their sinfulness is forgiven. This static and passive
description, however, is deepened and personalized in the second half of
the introduction. In fact, people are fortunate and happy if God does not
even *think* about them in terms of sinfulness or iniquity! The stanza ends
with the true purpose of the previous three lines: while transgressions may
be forgiven and sin may be covered, and while God's attitude is important,
these are all external to the person. The true result of these is found within
the person himself or herself: Such a person has no deceit, treachery, or
fraud about them.[17]

In the second stanza, which comprises verses 3–5, the psalmist gives a personal witness of the effect of living a life that is exactly opposite from that depicted in the introduction, and how that clear, open, and honest relationship was regained. As long as the psalmist had been silent, not recognizing or admitting the transgressions, sins, and iniquity mentioned in the introduction, his own bones—those parts of himself that are the strongest and most durable—began to wear out and become weak. Moreover, even when he screamed or raged[18] all the time, every day, day and night, God's hand—the thing that normally brings about deliverance and salvation—was pressing him down along with the sin. However, as soon as the psalmist recognizes his "sin...iniquity...transgressions" (paralleling the same terms in the introduction), God immediately forgives them and the relationship is completely restored.

In the third stanza, the psalmist takes his own experience and encourages others to learn from it. Those who are the recipients of God's faithfulness should always pray, always keeping that open and clear relationship in the forefront of their lives, neither being silent nor raging about their circumstances. By keeping that relationship honest and open, there is a type of protection and integrity for those who live in this way.

In the fourth stanza, which interrupts the flow of the psalm and appears in Hebrew more like prose than poetry, God speaks a direct warning to all those who hear the psalm: Do not be like stupid horses or donkeys. These animals have no understanding; they cannot learn from experience, either their own or that of others. They must be led around by force with a bit and reins. Without these implements, the animals will not even come near their owners. In other words, there is no open and honest relationship possible between these animals and those who care for them. The contrast with God's relationship with the psalmist and, furthermore, with all those who hear this psalm cannot be clearer.

In the final and concluding stanza of the psalm, the message and meaning of the introduction is repeated. Without an honest and open relationship between people and God, only pain and suffering are possible. But, conversely, when there is an open and honest relationship, faithfulness and trust continually envelop those who pursue it. As in the introduction, this environment and context of faithfulness and trust find a home in people: They become "upright" within their own selves.

Exodus 17:1–7: How Physical Deprivation Affects Our Spiritual Lives

[1] From the wilderness of Sin the whole congregation of the Israelites journeyed by stages, as the LORD commanded. They camped at Rephidim, but there was no water for the people to drink.

² The people quarreled with Moses, and said, "Give us water to drink." Moses said to them, "Why do you quarrel with me? Why do you test the LORD?" ³ But the people thirsted there for water; and the people complained against Moses and said, "Why did you bring us out of Egypt, to kill us and our children and livestock with thirst?" ⁴ So Moses cried out to the LORD, "What shall I do with this people? They are almost ready to stone me."

⁵ The LORD said to Moses, "Go on ahead of the people, and take some of the elders of Israel with you; take in your hand the staff with which you struck the Nile, and go. ⁶ I will be standing there in front of you on the rock at Horeb. Strike the rock, and water will come out of it, so that the people may drink." Moses did so, in the sight of the elders of Israel.

⁷ He called the place Massah and Meribah, because the Israelites quarreled and tested the LORD, saying, "Is the LORD among us or not?"

This small story is the fourth within a five-part series of stories in the Wilderness. The five are set within a chiastic structure: Israel is rescued from a foreign nation (Exod. 14:1–15:21); Israel is given water (15:22–27); Israel is given food (16:1–36); Israel is given water (17:1–7); Israel is rescued from a foreign nation (17:8–16). Therefore, when this story is read, it is difficult not to compare and contrast it with the parallel story in the pattern, the story of Marah (15:22–27). In both stories, Israel comes to a place where no potable water exists; they complain to Moses about the lack of water (and Moses' seeming bad leadership); Moses cries out to God; God gives instructions about solving the problem by using a piece of wood. Moreover, both stories have some reference to the name of the place and its significance, and both stories have the theme of "testing" as central to their meanings. On the other hand, while many differences between the stories appear, three are particularly significant.

First, in this story there is no actual scene where God provides water for the thirsty Israelites. When I read the story, I expect just that. The story seems to be set up in such a way that the suspense hinges upon the solution to the problem of the lack of water. The Israelites complain about the lack of water. They furthermore accuse Moses of wanting to kill them "with thirst" (17:3). Moses seems to think the lack of water is the cause of the problem as well. Finally, God gives detailed instructions–almost two whole verses in this tiny story–about how to provide water. When the climax actually occurs, I expect at least a few verses showing God's remarkable provision. Scenes of thirsty Israelites running for the huge stream coming from the rock. Episodes of them lapping and drinking and slurping, wading and playing and swimming in God's abundant gift. Perhaps even a short episode where the Israelites praise God as they did at the end of the Deliverance at the Sea (15:21). But, if that is my expectation, I am sorely disappointed. The climax of the story is related in eleven[19] words: "Moses did so, in the sight of the elders of Israel." It seems as if the point of the story is not, in fact, God's provision.

Second, the point of the story instead seems to be the theme introduced at Marah, the theme of testing. At Marah, God tested Israel to see if they could obey his instructions when and if he gave them. Here, however, the theme is not God testing Israel, but rather Israel testing God to see if he could, in fact, be trusted to take care of them. When faced with the possibility of their own deaths, Israel questions God's ability to be faithful to them.

Third, and finally, the narrator here employs a bit of revisionist history in order to make this point about the story as a whole. When the Israelites initially complain about their state, they say to Moses, "Give us water to drink!" (v. 2). When Moses shrugs off his responsibility, they continue, "Why did you bring us out of Egypt, to kill us and our children and livestock with thirst?" In other words, for Israel the problem is the lack of water and the dubious leadership ability of Moses. At the very end of the story, however, after God's instructions and Moses' response, after the naming of the place as Massah ("Test") and Meribah ("Trial"), the narrator seemingly reminds the reader what Israel had originally said as they complained earlier in the story. Here, however, the point is not about the lack of water or about Moses' dubious leadership. In the mind of the narrator, those complaints are beside the point. Whenever Israel complains over their state—whenever any one of us complain about our state—the narrator shows us what is at the heart of all those words: the Israelites quarreled and tested the LORD, saying, "Is the LORD among us or not?" Deprivation and lack, in the spiritual life, are never about the things we think we do not have or lack. Consistently, those complaints cut to the heart of our relationship with God and signal to us our own fears and insecurities about that relationship.

Preaching Series: Making Sense of the World in the Psalms

I have argued that the absence of the word or even concept of a "human body" in the Hebrew texts of the Bible is a clue to the fact that the usual, clear differentiation of reality between "me" and "everything else" is missing in the Old Testament worldview. This blurriness of human self-perception in the texts portrays a world in which there is a coherent and interdependent relationship between me as a human subject, the created world around me including other people and physical reality, and the God who is the source of it all. In such a world, paying attention to those ways that we know, perceive, and understand the world and God is especially important, because we humans are no longer simply observers on the world stage, but rather intimately interconnected with all that is. Our senses, in this understanding of what it means to be human, are not just gateways by which our brain or our "souls/spirits" receive information about the external world. Rather, they are the means by which I am connected to the world and the world is connected to me. Our five senses, according to the Old Testament, are not simply passive receptors of information but rather two-way paths by which I and all reality experience each other. This sermon series, therefore, takes a look at each of the five senses as they are represented in the book of Psalms, and tries to inquire how we can perceive and understand them differently and, perhaps, more helpfully.[20]

Sight

"Open my eyes, so that I may behold wondrous things out of your law." (Ps. 119:18)

Sight is the primary sense for most people. When faced with a new object or environment, most people rely on their sight first to understand it, followed by the other senses. Sight is so primary for most people that it is often assumed and rarely questioned as a true way of making sense of the world. This assumption, of course, can lead to the fascination with optical illusions and the entertainment of magic and sleight of hand. We accept that what we see is real and true, and this presumption sets us up for being tricked.

The verse from Psalm 119 above undercuts so many of our assumptions and presumptions about our eyesight. We think that it is something common, normal, usual. From the time that I first see daylight in the morning to the time that I close my eyes in sleep at night, I assume that what I see and, therefore, know about the world is true. But this verse undermines those two assumptions.

First, my eyes do not just open. While sight may or may not be a primary way in which I know the world, that sense is a gift from God. It is not I who opens my eyes to behold the world, but rather God. The verse assumes that, without God, my eyes remain closed and my perceptions of what is real are askew and shady.

Second, God does not open my eyes in order to live a humdrum existence, seeing all the usual, boring sights of my life. Eyes are not for seeing regular, tedious, dull things. No, when God is the opener of eyes, the result is an appreciation of wonder and majesty and beauty.

Hearing

"In your steadfast love hear my voice; O LORD, in your justice preserve my life." (Ps. 119:149)

Words are important. Being able to use words and appreciate the words of others are some of the foundational aspects of relating to other humans. Words are the basis of almost every relationship. The Hebrew word for "hear" is *shama*`. In English, "to hear" usually means simply to allow the ears to do what they do naturally. "I was sleeping so soundly, until I heard the alarm," we might say. Whether we want to or not, that buzzing, ringing sound makes its way into our ear canals and, whether we want it to or not, forces us awake.

Shama` is different, though. When in Deuteronomy 6 Israel is commanded to "Hear!... The LORD is our God alone," the people of God are not being told to simply open their ears to the droning babble of someone reading the sixth chapter of Deuteronomy. No, *shama*` here—and almost every other place in the Bible—isn't just "hearing" but "listening" or "paying attention to" or "noticing the significance of something" or "focusing attention on something." In a sense, while *shama*` is something one does with one's ears, it is more importantly something one does with one's mind. "Are you really hearing me?" we may ask a friend, meaning, "Do you understand, deeply, what I mean?"

Hearing is a sense that is closely tied to relationship. That relationship, in the book of Psalms, is illustrated perfectly in the way that God "hears our voice" when we cry or pray or weep or ask or plead or complain or laugh. We may ask God, "Are you really hearing me?" And consistently the answer is always "Yes, I deeply, completely understand what you mean, and who you are." God says, "I *shama*` you."

Smell

"Let my prayer be counted as incense before you, and the lifting up of my hands as an evening sacrifice." (Ps. 141:2)

Physiologically, the sense of smell is so closely located near the center of the brain that particular odors can bring back memories that have been buried and forgotten for decades. Nothing causes us to have a deep and lasting access to our world quite like smell. Odors in the Old Testament almost always accompany a developing relationship.

This is beautifully illustrated by two collections of material in the Bible. In the Song of Songs, the intimate, close relationship between the man and the woman is illustrated through the "fragrance" and "scent" of each other (1:3, 12; 2:13; 4:10–11; 7:9, 14). Moreover, the whole sacrificial system in the books of Leviticus and Numbers is understood as illustrating the close, intimate relationship between Israel and God. In dozens of passages, the sacrifices are described as a "pleasing odor to the LORD." While, of course, the blood of the sacrifices and the blood manipulation by the priests are important for the whole system, the sacrifices themselves are described in this very intimate way.[21]

Taste

"O taste and see that the LORD is good; happy are those who take refuge in him." (Ps. 34:8)

Eating and drinking are essential requirements for life. In this way, the sense of taste is different from the other four senses: all other senses are aspects of human life; taste is closely connected with maintaining life itself. Without food and drink, we die.[22] Having food and drink, we live, and taste is how we encounter those life-giving elements.

This fact cuts to the heart of Christian worship as it has come down to us from the very beginning. We meet together not only to sing, worship, hear readings, and listen to a reflection. We gather to eat together. With each other we engage in those basic activities that symbolize life: eating and drinking. Like Israel in the Wilderness, we are fed through God's own provision. And the wonderful thing about that life-giving provender is not just that it feeds our bellies; nor is it just that it feeds our souls. God's provision is marvelous because of its taste: "The house of Israel called it manna; it was like coriander seed, white, and the taste of it was like wafers made with honey" (Exod. 16:31). God not only provides us life but provides it to us abundantly—and tastily!

Touch

"If I take the wings of the morning
and settle at the farthest limits of the sea,
even there your hand shall lead me,
and your right hand shall hold me fast." (Ps. 139:9–10)

It can be argued that the sense of touch is the most important of all the other senses. While we may depend on sight while encountering unfamiliar things or situations, there is no other sense more closely connected with our intimate encounter with reality than touch. It is the first of the five senses to develop in the womb; touch is developed and activated in embryos at eight weeks of gestation. Furthermore, at the other end of the spectrum, it is the last of the senses that leave people when they die. Therapist Virginia Satir states that humans need four hugs a day to survive, eight hugs to maintain themselves, and twelve hugs to grow and flourish.

Touch is the way we make connections. In ancient Israel, the sacrifices that lay at the heart of Israel's relationship with God were activated through touch: "If the offering is a burnt offering from the herd, you shall offer a male without blemish; you shall bring it to the entrance of the tent of meeting, for acceptance in your behalf before the LORD. You shall lay your hand on the head of the burnt offering, and it shall be acceptable in your behalf as atonement for you" (Lev. 1:3–4). The animal can be brought; it can be checked; it can be slaughtered; it can be burnt. But none of these things personalize the sacrifice as affecting real people in real situations. Only when the worshipper touches the sacrifice, laying his or her hand on the head of the animal, only then is the sacrifice acceptable.

The use of the hand in touching in order to establish or continue a relationship does not occur only with humans. Ancient Israel also understood our relationship with God to be centered in God's hands touching us. God holds us, grasps us, guides us. God's hands are the central symbol of God's saving power.

In Isaiah 40, the image of God coming with power appears at first as an overwhelming presence. But when God appears in our midst, we note that God uses divine power, not to smite and overpower, but to tenderly care for the least of us:

See, the Lord GOD comes with might,
and his arm rules for him;
his reward is with him,
and his recompense before him.
He will feed his flock like a shepherd;
he will gather the lambs in his arms,
and carry them in his bosom,
and gently lead the mother sheep. (Isa. 40:10–11)

God's touch, like our touch, establishes and maintains relationship. And that touch may be overwhelming but, at the end of the day, we realize that it is only overwhelming in the care, passion, and love for each of us that it expresses.

7

Moses Meets Main Street:
The Media Are the Message–
Old Testament Themes in Film

By Richard Stern

As you open the door, a blast of frigid air prods you to rush back to the car and get the sweater you had thrown in the backseat because it is always so cold at the mall theater. After retrieving the sweater, you return for this Sunday afternoon's get-out-of-the-house junket. The smell of popcorn is almost irresistible, but you manage to settle for a box of Dots. Into the theater you go, find a seat, and suffer through the interminable trailers for upcoming films. Finally, the opening credits roll, the lion roars, and off you go at the movies.

What you have just done might be called escape, entertainment, even enlightenment; it all depends on the movie, of course, not to mention your state of mind, body, and spirit. But it is also an unwitting act of enculturation: subtle, pervasive, unrelenting enculturation. Bernard Brandon Scott proposes more modestly that "[w]e propagate our myths in films and TV programs."[1] Some would go further and label it a religious activity. As John Lyden contends, "There is no absolute distinction between religion and other aspects of culture, and that we have a tendency to label certain sorts of activities as 'religious' chiefly because they fall into the patterns that we recognize from religions with which we are familiar."[2] This example of blurred categories is evident in the old movie theaters that were constructed as Egyptian temples with sculptures of Egyptian gods hanging hither and yon and, on the other hand, churches that have taken over movie theaters or new church structures that are constructed as huge auditoriums nearly devoid of religious symbols. Lyden further defines religion as "a 'myth' or story that conveys a worldview; a set of values that idealizes how the world should be; and a ritual expression that unites the two."[3] Historically, the media for this propagation have been sacred writings, legends, and storytelling. Today, it is films. Nearly from film's beginnings, film and Scripture have had a close relationship, sometimes comfortable and other times not. Yet, the Bible maintains its own enduring influence on culture via the movies. As Adele Reinhartz notes, "movies attest to the Bible's role in shaping the ways in which we tell our stories, mold our heroes, understand our experience, imagine our future, and explain ourselves to ourselves."[4]

Film and Culture

According to many observers, film (along with television) has largely usurped the role of other cultural and sacred artifacts as the medium of choice for embedding the cultural values and stories that both reflect and shape those who view the films. "Film has become our Western culture's major storytelling and myth-producing medium."[5] Even beyond the usurpation of scriptures by film, Clive March claims, "*Entertainment is taking the place of religion as a cultural site where the task of meaning making is undertaken.*"[6] We used to sit around the campfires or in temples and tell stories about the ancients: how creation happened; how we came to inhabit the Promised Land; how Uncle Otto moved from Germany to escape the call of the Kaiser; how the grandmothers once got tipsy at the family Christmas Eve gathering. We have heard the stories recited again and again. We *tell* the stories again and again. You have surely noticed that when someone asks, "Did I tell you about the time …?" and you acknowledge that they have, they retell the story anyway. We needed to tell the stories maybe even more than we needed to hear them. Of course, the stories evolve some over time as they are modified to fit each new situation and as the storyteller changes over time. Different facets of the story come into play.

After millennia of telling stories, we started painting them on cave walls and writing the stories down or so that others might know the stories, too. Eventually, we began collecting them in books, reading them for ourselves or out loud to our kids. Even though the kids could recite the stories *exactly* as they were written, they wanted to hear them again. And again. And again. Such is the power of story. But the stories didn't change so much anymore. In writing them down they became more fixed, less elastic. And little Darla would let you know in no uncertain terms if you misread the story. Their lessons buried themselves in our consciousness and in our consciences, forging embedded plotlines and interpretive, hermeneutical structures for us to employ as we grew up: stories of courage, forgiveness, faith, and more. We got an image of the characters and the places in our minds. Some of the stories, the events, and the characters became so important that they took on normative, even sacred, stature.

But each time the story was told, even the written ones, it came out a little differently: a slip of the tongue, a different word emphasized, a longer pause. Not so with film, with the recent exception of "director's cuts," outtake offerings, and alternate endings that come packaged with the DVD. We have become less likely to tell the stories than to let others, mostly corporate communication conglomerates, tell them to us via film. We may blithely offer some commentary about the film on the way home or at the water cooler the next day or over lunch, but the process of imaging has largely been ceded to film. We sit in movie theaters, letting the over-sized images and the deep, thumping tsunami of sound wash over us, massaging (or hammering) our brains into submission. We don't have to imagine the scenes ourselves anymore. The images have been provided in over-sized, computerized, high-definition, and now 3D renditions. Moses will eternally look like Charlton Heston, or is it the other way around? Even though attendance figures seem to have reached a plateau, overall movie revenues are up and the hits just keep on happenin'. The problem with film or any medium that fixes the story is that the story can lose its adaptability to adapt to evolving cultural realities and challenges. The corrective in film is to do sequels (even prequels as in the *Star Trek* and *Star Wars* series), or newer versions of the same story, such as DeMille's 1923 and 1956 versions of *The Ten Commandments* or, more recently, *True Grit*, which came out in 1969 with iconic John Wayne starring and then again in 2010 with Jeff Bridges in the starring role of the Coen brothers production, both films based on a Charles Portis novel (1968).

The movies "function as a primary source of power and meaning for people throughout the world. Along with the church, the synagogue, the mosque, and the temple, they often provide people with stories through which they can understand their lives."[7] Scott similarly notes, the "movies and television shows are our modern myths; through them we work out who we are and negotiate the problems of modern life."[8] We have more and more venues in which to engage these culture-carving juggernauts: movie theaters, IMAX theaters, home theaters, movies on my computer, and cell phone, iPad, anywhere, anytime on DVD, Hulu, Roku, Blu-Ray, Netflix, Hot picks, Red Box, cable and satellite, streamed by wired and wireless channels. Even if one were somehow never to actually watch a movie, the impact of the movies would be impossible to avoid or deny with omnipresent television reviews, celebrity interviews, magazine articles, billboards, blogs, product tie-ins, and the like. I could, and many seem to be attempting to, navigate life nearly without ever looking away from some screen or another: cell or smart phone, television, computer, GPS, tablet, etc. Life for many has become mediated through LCD and LED screens, large and small. This cannot help but have an impact on our perception of reality. Indeed, each medium, even each screen, has its own particular impact on our perception of the information as well as the value of the information it conveys. Think Marshall McLuhan. What is a person, what is a preacher, to do in the face of all this? Become a Luddite or install multiple projectors and screens in the sanctuary? Rejection or competition? Is there a middle ground, a happy medium?

Some religious folks have suggested avoiding altogether contemporary media and the culture in which it resides. Think Amish. At the other extreme, others have whole-heartedly employed contemporary media to their own often religiously conservative purposes, whether radio, television, Internet, or film. Others yet suggest a more moderate reaction with boycotts of media with objectionable content or occasional planned media fasts for an hour, a day, or for a season. Or how about media appointments, that is, actually *choosing* to watch something on television, not just watching because that big screen on the wall has been glowing since the kids came home after school?[9] Some attempt to employ the various media but naively fill them with content they hope will counteract the commercial stuff they decry, as though the medium itself had no influence on the message. It is, in any case, a hopeless cause to deny or try to escape the pervasive influence of film in our culture, our values, and even our vision of how things are and/or ought to be. According to Michael Warren, "Images, in conjunction with their validating contexts, tend to influence us with a power all the greater as we are less aware."[10]

The best we can do then is become savvy participants. The savvier we become, the less gullible we become, and the less susceptible we are to the pervasive messages being deployed. Gordon Lynch observes, "If cinemagoing [sic] is indeed a significant ritual framework for engaging with meaning-laden narratives, then we need to understand more about what audiences bring to and from such rituals if we are to have a fuller understanding of how films genuinely function as transmitters of cultural ideologies in people's experience."[11] Further, "theologians need to turn their attention from a pure focus on film texts to the ways in which people make use of films in their own personal, meaning-making activities."[12] On the other side of the equation, John Lyden cautions, "We fail to acknowledge the extent to which modern people base their worldviews and ethics upon sources we do not usually label 'religious.' Though we may see the powers of the new media, we often fear them and do not wish to recognize them as sharing in the same functions that historically have accorded to religion."[13]

What's at stake is, at minimum, the matter of control. The one who controls the channels of communication ultimately controls the content on the channels. Who controls the images that bombard me? What is their text and subtext? How can I arm myself against any insidious influence they might impart? How do I as a preacher engage them meaningfully, ethically? What is my relationship to these cultural artifacts? How do Scripture and film dialog with one another? Is dialog even possible? Can I employ movies in my preaching? What are the risks and opportunities? These and a cascading series of additional questions confront the preacher who hopes to engage the medium of film and any Old (and New) Testament themes. Bernard Brandon Scott warns, "If we do not develop an awareness, literacy, and objectivity about our new media, understand their epistemology, and formulate a hermeneutics of Bible translation in the new media, then religion will become entertainment."[14] I would contend this is already the case and was foreshadowed decades ago when, as noted earlier, movie theaters were constructed to resemble exotic temples and places of worship. Now many new churches are constructed like movie theaters: huge auditoriums with comfortable raked seating and big projection screens dominating the front of the church with nary a religious symbol in sight, except for the offering plate. The assembly has become an audience observing the spectacle of worship. Woods and Patton in *Prophetically Incorrect* claim that "popular media create simple stories and characters with values that most people can relate to. In a priestly sense, these stories reinforce common values and affirm what audiences want to believe about their own tribe's superiority."[15] The key here is "want to believe" as opposed to "need to hear." Films tend to reinforce what we already believe rather than move us to belief or modify our belief.

Film and Scripture

For the purposes of this essay, we now need to zoom our hermeneutic lens in a bit to see how Scripture, the Old Testament in particular, interacts with this medium called film. Oddly perhaps, the close study of the Old Testament prepares us in many ways for the study of film, with the reverse being true as well. It depends on one's starting point. Remarkably, both employ many of the same tactics based on similar intuitions and assumptions. First, we hear or read stories, including Old Testament stories, and watch films with the assumption that they have a plot; that they are more than just a random sequence of events without purpose or direction. As the various characters interact, the plot moves along toward its end with occasional disruptive plot twists that seem, at least temporarily, to derail the plot. Even as there is suspense at wondering how the story will unfold, we assume a deeper confidence that all the loose ends will come together at the close of the story. If this does not happen, the story and the film are deemed unsatisfactory. Even non-narrative passages generally exist within larger narrative contexts.

Second, both film and Scripture are generally assumed to operate on multiple levels, that is, beyond the literal or surface meaning. We read Bible stories as having layered meanings, moral implications, and life lessons; they point to something or someone beyond the surface operation of the event being reported. We can easily apply the ancient levels of literary interpretation (literal, allegorical, tropological, and anagogical) to film analysis.[16] Poetry and hymns evoke consideration of loftier meaning than mere descriptive *reportage*. We are quick to ask, "What does that poem *mean?*" Or, "What was that film *about?*" These forms aim to create an experience in the reader/listener/viewer. They operate out of Aristotle's *The Poetics* rather than *The Rhetoric*. We might ask, for example, with whom do I identify in a film? What does the film set in motion in my emotional life; what touches me in the film; what memories or desires are triggered? How am I even marginally different for having watched the film or read the story or Bible passage? The film and the Scripture passage do not exist only in order for me to ask about my identity, of course, but they may well provoke such reflections. We are moved to reflect beyond the film's surface functioning as mere storytelling. The stories, the Scriptures, and the films all function as platforms from which additional and deeper forays into meaning are launched.

Third, the study of the Old Testament should also clue us in to the idea of the editing of a literary artifact that has been consciously, thoughtfully, and purposefully assembled from many parts and influences. This would be the case with the Bible as a whole but also with each of its constituent books. The toolbox of Scripture studies has expanded to include a host of scholarly *Geschichtes*, with *Redaktion Geschichte* or redaction analysis as just one example. How has an author redacted—borrowed and then stitched together—the various separate components of the narrative into an approximate whole? Scripture, as a book and as a book made up of many books, is a product resulting, in part, from a process of gathering diverse writings, viewpoints, events, and characters, and trying to create some sort of thematic or narrative unity from all the parts, maintaining all the while respect for the several perspectives and even different versions of the same event; the creation story is one example. Biblical editors, in fashioning their works, had to decide, whether by divine inspiration, editorial judgment, or some combination, what to incorporate and what to leave out as they collated and re-fashioned these many materials. There was serious and thoughtful editing to be done. After thorough study, one begins to notice the particular preferences and stylistic characteristics of a biblical author in comparison to another—Luke as opposed to Matthew, for example, or the JEPD editors in the Pentateuch as another. The careful reader may even venture a speculation about motives for the choices that were made. One might well do the same with movie directors by sampling their work. What ties the work of the author/editor together? What patterns emerge?

With the study of Scripture then, particularly the Old Testament, we develop an appreciation for levels of meaning, for multiple perspectives contained within one overarching narrative, and for the need to interpret the material we are engaging in order to do it justice. Is a story just a story? In both film and Scripture, authors have needed to edit material to form a seemingly organic narrative, recognizing the importance of plot in creating and sustaining interest. The next critical question might be, how does the choice of medium impact the message? The medium that conveys the narrative has its own constraints and values. Biblical authors employed story, hymn, parable, and other literary forms to nuance the presentation of their works. Each mode works differently on the hearer/reader. Each has an embedded set of inherent values, likewise in modern, electronic media. Computers, for example, move us to conclude that accessing vast amounts of data and fast processing that data are good things. Cell phones assume that being constantly accessible is a good thing. High-definition conveys that ever higher resolution is a good thing. Yet sometimes a soft-focus lens is employed to soften that ultra-sharp detail. Movies generally expand images to larger-than-life size in excruciating detail, making shots of grand vistas optimal. Television, in contrast, is the medium of close-ups. The characteristics of a medium, both opportunities and limitations, shape the conveyed message and consequently the experience of the viewer/listener.

While the close studies of film and of Scripture can be mutually illuminating, there is an intervening and complicating factor: intertextuality. What happens when a text is converted from one medium of transmission or presentation into another? Something is inevitably and unavoidably added and something lost. After all, to an important degree, context determines content. The medium which conveys the message influences the message conveyed. This goes back to Marshall McLuhan and the idea that the medium is really the message.[17] McLuhan's popularity seems to ebb and flow with the tides, but he makes important points that seem to recur every decade or so.

The central question has been, how accurately has the message been translated as it moves from one medium to the other? But this concern for translating the literary artifact into film with accuracy or integrity may have drifted to the margins as a goal. Critics are more likely to look at the other aspects of the film without significant reference to the original artifact. In the case of a movie based on a book, an overriding question initially was how faithfully does the film reproduce or re-present the book? But this changed or evolved. Guerric DeBona notes, "the key dynamic in understanding the struggle for authorship in adaptation lies precisely in comprehending the shift from an interest in the text to the director as new author, after the Second World War."[18] And then later, "the auteurists came to admire the director not because of his successful literary translation, but precisely because he showcased *performance*, which over and over trumped *literary translation*."[19]

As one example of this matter of intertextuality, it is important to recall that most of the films that come to mind when considering Old Testament themes and film were produced in Hollywood—which is to say, they are imbued with a western, even an American perspective and are probably, either by default or design, promoting western, American values underneath the film's plot, none of which may be the values embedded in the scriptural original. The Bible becomes subservient to American cultural values rather than challenging them. God always seems to promote freedom and democracy. Gordon Lynch notes more expansively the "general values of contemporary Hollywood film, which celebrates personal freedom, compassion, intimacy, courage, expressiveness, creativity, individuality, and authenticity."[20] To employ films, whether in teaching or preaching, as some sort of neutral, values-free medium for biblical catechesis is an enormous mistake and recklessly naïve. First, the process of adapting a literary text to film requires, as we have already noted, a great deal of decision-making by many, many individuals, each with a vested interest in the outcome of the film. Hermeneutics is inevitably involved in deciding, not only what to include and exclude from the scriptural original, but in how to portray and employ what is included: camera angles, characterization, costume, scene selection, all those things that comprise *mise-en-scene*, which shape the resulting product as well as the message and values the product may intend to convey. This is simply part of the problem or situation of intertextuality—moving from one form of text to another, from one medium to another.

Yet another interesting dimension of this matter of intertextuality comes to play. Craig Detweiler offers an interesting speculation:

> The ancient tension between the sovereignty of God and the free will of his people informs the filmmaking process. Some directors prefer a predetermined cinematic universe, where artistic decisions are made months before film rolls. Others create an open atmosphere, where actors are free to improvise, to serve as co-directors of the project. Perhaps the differences in directors' styles correspond to their understanding of human nature and audience behavior. Is the audience something to be respected or directed, cajoled or corralled? Are actors just props at the director's disposal, a means to a manipulative end? Or is the filmmaker called upon to serve the story (and the audience)? These questions have echoes in the debate about humanity's role in the Garden of Eden. Does dominion over nature allow us to exploit it or is our role comparable to caretaker, tending the garden with the utmost respect?[21]

The dynamic of intertextuality is simply unavoidable. And therein lies the danger of a naïve appropriation of scriptural themes in film. The danger is that we operate as though the film is a sort of one-to-one transfer of meaning from Scripture to film, assuming in the process that the film's rendition of the Scripture passage is values neutral or that they share the same values system if they are portraying the same biblical event or character. Even though, on the surface, they might seem to tell the same story, the medium is the message. The medium of film promotes a different vision. The film turns everything in its frame into something bigger than life as it decontextualizes its subject matter.[22] A film will likely say a great deal more about the time and culture in which it was produced than about the Old Testament story it portrays. A 1950s film, *The Ten Commandments* (1956), for example, is inescapably a mid-twentieth century artifact reflecting mid-twentieth century values and interests. One should be extremely cautious about assuming any direct correspondence between scriptural accounts and cinematic versions of the same events or characters. One is *always* dealing with someone else's "take" on a biblical story.

Old Testament Themes

Let's zoom in yet a little more and look at the interplay between the Old Testament and film. There are a couple of angles one could take here. One could merely look at how Old Testament events have been portrayed in film. This is an old story in the history of film. Many of the very earliest silent as well as later talking films employed biblical content for their subject material in order to acquire credibility for this new medium as something of a serious nature, more than novelty, entertainment, and diversion. As DeBona notes, "the use of the canonical was a shrewd marketing tool in early cinema."[23] Scripture was a ready source for plotlines with which viewers were presumably familiar. Biblical epics were a Hollywood staple for decades. *David and Bathsheba* (1951), *Samson and Delilah* (1949), *The Ten Commandments*, and others exemplify the persistent attraction of biblical material, especially biblical characters, for films. The audience could be presumed to be able to fill in details that the film director had to leave on the cutting room floor. In the current state of relative biblical illiteracy, one would not dare to assume this today. The images these films projected became as iconic as the Scripture passages they sought to dramatize. Perhaps the exemplar for this cinematic approach is Cecil B. DeMille's *The Ten Commandments* in its two versions, 1923 and 1956.

One might also keep a score sheet based on biblical references, quotations, and allusions within a "secular" film. *True Grit* (2010), for example, contains numerous Old Testament quotations and allusions, which, while not driving the primary plotline, do provide a running commentary on the interaction of the characters and their motives as the plot moves along.

An approach with greater scope and far richer and more provocative content than the overt portrayal of biblical characters and events is to take major themes that course through the Old Testament and find analogies in secular films, seeing how the themes play out persistently in film and how they are portrayed in extra-biblical contexts. Of course, the Old Testament is a screenwriter's treasure chest of themes: adultery, betrayal, sex, salvation, redemption, theodicy, and murder. Walter Brueggemann, in his *Reverberations of Faith: A Theological Handbook of Old Testament Themes*, offers a list of 105 themes he explores in alphabetical order. Some of these are proper names of persons and places, which might not help us too much in this discussion.[24] Others, however, are indeed helpful. A short list (with film possibilities) might include: apocalyptic thought (*Independence Day*, among many others), atonement (*Crazy Heart*), blessing, community (*Lars and the Real Girl*), covenant, creation, death, election, ethics, exile, faith, the Fall (*American Beauty*), forgiveness, hope, image of God (*Oh God, Oh God II*), land, listening, love, Messiah (*Cool Hand Luke*), money (*Wall Street, Wall Street: Money Never Sleeps*), neighbor, promise, redemption (*Crazy Heart, Joe versus the Volcano, The Truman Show*), repentance, sexuality (*Fatal Attraction* and a host of others), sin, suffering (*A Serious Man, Cape Fear*), violence, war (*Saving Private Ryan*), wilderness.

Adele Reinhartz' book *Scripture on the Silver Screen* explores just these sorts of connections. In each of eleven chapters, she explores a film and the theme(s) she gleans, mostly from the Old Testament. For example, in chapter 1, she explores *The Truman Show* via the theme of "leave-taking," as in leaving home but also as in leaving the Garden of Eden. "The Bible presents so many examples of this theme that such departures must surely have been a feature of ancient Israelite society as well."[25] *Pleasantville* might then be viewed as the complex of illusions we create to convince ourselves that we are still in Eden and just how illusory the result is. Each chapter summarizes the film under consideration and then moves to an extended comparison with biblical text(s): plot, character, and evident themes as manifested in the movie.

Several recent films that some critics have associated with the Old Testament book of Job include *Signs* (2002), a science fiction film that was written, produced, and directed by M. Night Shyamalan.[26] Another is *A Serious Man* (2009), a work of the brothers Joel and Ethan Coen. The film portrays the life of a husband/father/college teacher whose life is marked by relentless misfortune. A third film is *Cape Fear*, the story of a killer's attempt at revenge on his lawyer. These are very different stories and would seem at the surface to have little in common. All, however, raise the questions of moral ambiguity and of whether or not God is involved in our human affairs. Douglas E. Cowen notes in a discussion about another science fiction film, but also about science fiction in general, "Very often, what we fear most is not the absence of the gods, but their apathy. We are afraid that they are there, somewhere, but that they just don't care."[27] This would seem to be a theme consistent with the concerns of Job. Job kept faith but not without a struggle. The various claims about 9/11 and hurricane Katrina being God's punishment suggest this remains a relevant theme. Is God active in our lives, and if so how?

Scripture, Film, and the Task of Preaching

Remarkably, except for the difference in elapsed time and expense involved, the flow of activities for creating scriptural texts, for making a film based on or referring to those scriptural texts, and for preparing to preach from scriptural texts is not all that different. The same basic schematic is in place. All three–Scripture, film, and preaching–have climbed a similar ladder of steps from inspiration to implementation. The practitioners paddle around in the reservoir of universal ideas, experiences, hopes, and fears until some idea coalesces and emerges from the miasma. They all then create a tentative plot or structure that will contain and advance that basic idea and its sub points. Next, they choose language and images to communicate the idea and the plot to the intended viewer/listener. Editing the sources to fit the plot comes next. Finally, there is the presentation of the end product, with the hope that there will be some positive response. In preaching as in film, the matter of intertextuality is omnipresent: how will the scriptural text be modified, whether by design or by default, simply by its translation into the medium of preaching?

In accord with the dynamic of intertextuality with Scripture and film, the goal in preaching is to convert biblical energy into homiletic energy. One of David Buttrick's definitions or goals of preaching is to recreate the intention of a text's intention. He asks the preacher to consider not just what a text might mean but what a text does.[28] In other words, the preacher is trying to capture something from the medium of Scripture and carry that core "something" into another medium–preaching. As with any such activity, signal or message distortion is probable, really inevitable. Even as a lector recites a passage from the lectionary during the worship service, the process of "coloring" or interpreting the text is occurring: which words and how words are emphasized, where pauses are inserted, etc. There is no way of avoiding this, except perhaps for a Vulcan mind-meld.

With regard to the matter of plotted language, my colleague Fr. Guerric DeBona, OSB, writes pointedly about the importance of plot in preaching: "the preacher who finds a plot usually finds direction, unity, and intention in the homily." He then enumerates five reasons for using "plot-like structure" in a homily. Plots are: (1) organic, (2) focus on the listener, (3) drive toward closure, (4) create tension, and (5) mirror God's master plot, or the way the tradition reads the story of salvation.[29] "At its sharpest the sermon functions like a work of fiction, taking us 'by faith' into a world in which a claim is made which is accepted as true inasmuch as we are persuaded to believe it to be so, and that persuasion can be of many kinds, intellectual, emotive, aesthetic or moral."[30]

So, then, how can the preacher make use of the plentiful material, whether as content or model, offered to us in film? First, I urge great caution if the preacher plans to use film clips in sermons. It could work well in a retreat setting, but not, except for assiduous, careful planning, on Sunday morning in the middle of the liturgy! The film clip will likely kidnap the occasion. It takes sermon time to set it up and the process bogs the sermon down, not to mention the rest of the liturgy. Additionally, the technology usually chooses to malfunction at the most inopportune moments. As a former audio/video producer, I know this firsthand. I have seen a film clip used only once effectively, but numerous times ineffectively. As Timothy Cargal puts it, "When employing a film as a dialogue partner in preaching, how do we keep the film from running away with the sermon?"[31] Later he opines, "One seemingly obvious way to bring film into dialogue with preaching would be to show a key scene that encapsulates the movie's theme rather than trying to relate it orally. I will just come right out and say it that this is a fundamentally bad idea."[32] Of course, others have quite different opinions and experiences on this matter of film clips in sermons. The goal, in any case, should never be simply to use a film clip in order to seem "with it" or contemporary, or to use the latest technology just because you have it. Film clips are merely a means, not an end, and not always the most effective means. After papyrus and velum, you, the preacher, are the most effective, enduring mass medium yet invented. The preacher certainly can use brief descriptions of plots, scenes, interaction of characters, and even quote short segments of dialog. This way the preacher employs the dynamic of the scene and yet the situation is completely in the preacher's control.

Films provide us with innumerable examples of those themes that flow through the Old Testament: humanity writ large as played out on the silver screen: foibles, forgiveness, destiny, strength, weakness, and so on. As a preacher, one thing I value about the Old Testament is the depth of its characters. This may be a C.L.M. (Career Limiting Move), but I confess that I find New Testament characters rather two-dimensional in comparison to the folks who reside in the Old Testament. The Old Testament characters are richer, more textured, and more vivid. I find them easier to relate to, people I might like to meet, even if I might not actually like them. As a result, I find it easier to present and employ Old Testament characters in preaching. This suggests something for us as preachers. As we sketch characters and events in our preaching, they need to be vivid, real, believable, not cardboard cutouts. Writers employ the dictum: show it; don't tell it. Give us more than a label; give us some detail so we can picture the scene, the character. Both the Old Testament and film teach us about the importance of developing rich characters, people we find interesting, who have depth and to whom we can relate. Both Old Testament and film teach us about the importance of plot in preaching, a sense of going somewhere, of having some destination such that we keep paying attention. We learn about the importance of rich characterization, making the abstract concrete, real.

One final caution: Film should never be used as a substitute for Scripture itself simply because the film rendition might seem more interesting or lively or entertaining. Film might be better employed to contrast our cultural values with those of the Scriptures, even as they both intend to portray the same event or character. The quest should be, as Cargal frames it, "[H]ow can films be used to make explicit those cultural assumptions so that they may be brought into dialogue with Scripture and Christian faith?"[33] This is the hermeneutical circle at work: While we interpret the Scripture, as well as film and preaching, they also interpret us. Or, in something of a reversal of direction, Reinhartz urges that "those of us who regularly read and study biblical literature should worry about those for whom popular culture is the primary vehicle for biblical knowledge. Our mission, should we choose to accept it, is to help others to an educated reading of the text against which movies and other popular representations of the Bible may be tested."[34] Amen to that.

8

Poets of the Word:
Using Literature as
Sermon Resource

By Ruthanna B. Hooke

One of the ways that the Old Testament has influenced our culture is through the extraordinary effusion of literature, poetry, and plays that make use of themes and stories from these Hebrew Scriptures. This literature provides a rich trove of interpretation of these texts. Since the preacher is also in the business of interpreting biblical texts, it makes sense that this literature would serve as an outstanding resource for sermons. John Holbert's preaching demonstrates the many ways that this resource can be used with grace, humor, and insight. This essay offers some considerations and guidelines for preachers who want to follow Holbert's fine example and use literary resources in sermons. As promising as this practice is, using literature in sermons is complicated and requires thought. I will begin by considering these challenges through an exploration of the purposes of literature and their relationship to the purposes of sermons. This theoretical exploration will provide the framework for offering some guidelines for the use of this material to good effect in sermons. In the second part of this essay I pair lectionary texts with poems based on these texts, suggesting ways that these poems offer surprising and stimulating interpretations of these texts that can spark the preacher's imagination. In the third part of this essay I propose a sermon series on the Genesis Creation accounts (Gen. 1:1–2:25), which draws on the wealth of poetry that has been written on this topic.

It should be noted that preachers who use literature in sermons often use literature that does not explicitly comment on scripture. Novels, poetry, and plays, by their very nature as works of art, comment on the nature of reality and human existence, seeking to make meaning of it. Since the preacher too seeks to make meaning of life, it makes sense that he or she would turn to these literary resources, tapping the insights of others who have struggled with this task of understanding and depicting our lives. Literature of all sorts can thus be profitably used in sermons. Although the reflections I offer on the sermonic use of literature can apply to any literature used, this essay largely focuses on using literature that explicitly comments on scripture passages from the Old Testament.

There are a variety of ways that literature can be used in sermons. One common practice is to use a story from fiction, such as a novel, play, or short story, as a sermon illustration. For this practice, many of the same considerations that govern any use of sermon illustrations—such as whether they illuminate or distract from the biblical text, whether they require too much background to be helpful, whether they are culturally accessible to the congregation—would govern decisions about how to use illustrations chosen from literature. Another practice is to include the literary work itself in the sermon, and chiefly this means using a poem as part of the sermon, since most fictional works are too long to fit into the standard sermon length. This essay will focus on this second practice, since this raises particular questions about the relationship between the sermon and the artwork embedded in it.

Part I – The Use of Literature in Sermons:

Considerations and Guidelines

To use literature in a sermon is to embed one kind of work (the piece of literature) into another kind of work (a sermon). This will be successful only if the two kinds of work have similar or at least complementary purposes, otherwise the two pieces of work will undermine each other to the detriment of both. Thus, to see how well literature can work in sermons and serve the preaching task, it is useful to ask what the purpose of literature is compared to the purpose of sermons. Because literature is an art form, it shares the purposes or *raison d'etre* of all art. Naming the purposes of art allows us to see the similarities and differences between art's purposes—what art is and what it is trying to do—and those of the sermon—what sermons are, and what they are trying to do. Because the purposes of these two kinds of work differ in certain respects, there may well be tension in using literature in a sermon since the artwork enclosed in the sermon may have a different goal than the sermon itself. This tension can either undermine or enhance the sermon, but it is important for preachers to understand that this tension exists so they can use it creatively. Thus, understanding the similarities and differences between the purposes of literature and of the sermon creates a framework for investigating the challenges of using literature in sermons as well as the benefits of doing so.

While it is notoriously difficult to define art or to name its purposes, theologians and theorists offer some guidance. Rowan Williams's exploration of the nature and purposes of art suggests that the deep similarities between sermons and artworks are rooted in the common motives that spur artists to create and preachers to preach. Williams describes the artist's urge to create as beginning with the awareness of something unfinished in ordinary perception; the artist is aware that "things are not only what they are, and give more than they have."[1] Our conceptual forms do not exhaustively capture the "what" of what is known. There is an excess in the object known, as it has its own life. Artists seek to explore this life of the object and then set it free into the world. Artists are looking for the deeper patterns and pulsions of things: "Art moves from and into a depth in the perceptible world that is contained neither in routine perception nor in the artist's conscious or unconscious purposes."[2] Hence the purpose of art is not simply to reproduce items of ordinary consciousness but to reveal a deeper reality in them. In order to do this, the artist simultaneously devotes a "highly specific attention to what is given," while at the same time seeks to "'thin out' the given materiality so as to re-embody what it is that is given and yet eludes the original embodiment."[3] This attention to the givenness of the created world, while at the same time seeking out the depth dimension of this world, links art-making to sacramental ways of seeing the world, which also discern a deeper, sacred reality to ordinary objects. As Flannery O'Connor puts it, the artistic mind is one that "is willing to have its sense of mystery deepened by contact with reality, and its sense of reality deepened by contact with mystery."[4] Art opens us to God by opening us to the real. It is in attending to both reality and mystery, O'Connor argues, that artists arrive at insights into the nature of the world that are deeply true, thus making meaning of our existence.

Like artists, preachers too seek to articulate deeper truths about reality than are perceived superficially, while at the same time remaining grounded in the givenness and reality of the world. In this double task, preachers also engage in sacramental perception, seeking to reveal the depth dimension of reality and to make meaning of it, while at the same time honoring the materiality and givenness of that reality. In this sense the preacher's task is like that of the artist, and the sermon is similar to an artwork in what it seeks to express about the world, and how it seeks to express it. Inasmuch as sermons and artworks share these similar motivations and purposes, the use of literature in a sermon can enhance the sermon, since both the literature embedded in the sermon and the sermon enclosing it are trying to accomplish similar ends.

Williams's theological aesthetics, however, also suggests some dissimilarities between the nature and purposes of art and those of the sermon. He notes that the purpose of art-making is to aim for the good of what is made rather than some other good that is separable from the artwork, even if that be the good of humanity.[5] His description of art-making draws on Flannery O'Connor's statement that art is something that is "valuable in itself and that works in itself."[6] As O'Connor puts it, a work of art must "carry its meaning inside it"; the meaning of the artwork must be conveyed by the work itself, not by a message that can be separated from the work. For instance, she argues that the novelist cannot make an inadequate story work by putting a statement of its meaning on the end of it.[7] Drawing on O'Connor's criteria for art, Williams defines propaganda as a work in which the message of the work is separable from the work itself, or in which the message of the work is known beforehand because the work itself aims to express a particular ideology.[8]

These descriptions of the purpose of art suggest the ways in which sermons are distinct from art. Unlike the artist, the preacher is not only concerned with the good of what is made (the sermon itself), but is also concerned with edifying hearers and converting them. The purpose of literature is to achieve the goodness of the work itself, whereas sermons have another purpose, which is to convey a certain message and achieve a certain effect. While literature, as an art form, is loyal only to itself, the sermon has to be loyal to the Gospel, to present truths that are consonant with this Good News. This means that the preacher will always have a message that is separable from the sermon itself, a message that is known beforehand–the basic *kerygma* of the Gospel, which has to be the focus of every sermon. In a sense, all sermons are propaganda as they aim to express a particular "ideology"–the Christian faith–that must govern and guide any artfulness in the sermon. According to Williams' criteria, an artist who had this motivation would betray the goodness of what is made by focusing on something external to the work itself.

Another way to locate the difference in purpose between sermons and literature is that, while sermons are artful or are an art, they are not "works of art." Nicholas Wolterstorff defines a work of art as "an entity made or presented to serve as object of aesthetic contemplation."[9] A work of art is a painting you gaze at in a museum or a piano recital you listen to in a hushed concert hall. As Don Saliers points out, while there may be contemplative elements in liturgy, the purpose of the liturgy is for the participants to contemplate God rather than the liturgy itself or any element within it, such as the sermon.[10] The participants use or engage in the liturgy, not as an end in itself, but as a vehicle for encounter with God. Thus, in this sense also, the sermon does not stand alone nor does it function as an end in itself; rather, it is meant to be employed as a means toward communion with God. This differentiates the sermon from a work of art, which means to function as an end in itself, and becomes propaganda when it seeks to fulfill a purpose outside of its own integrity or excellence.

These differences between a sermon's purpose and that of an artwork suggest that using artwork in a sermon could create tension in the sermon. The piece of literature, and the sermon in which it is embedded, could be directed toward two divergent goals–the piece of literature directed toward the good of the artwork itself, and the sermon directed toward the proclamation of the Good News. One way for the preacher to address this tension is to be careful that the literature used is compatible with the Good News she seeks to share. As Don Saliers notes, since Christian faith orients itself around the paschal mystery–the life, death, and resurrection of Jesus Christ–the continuing enactment of that mystery in Christian liturgy "both requires and continually judges the aesthetics brought to the liturgy," including those of the sermon. Saliers continues: "The arts brought to the liturgical assembly are necessary and must be assessed not on purely aesthetic grounds, as with 'works of art.' Rather, they are subject to the inner paradox Christian liturgy celebrates: the kenotic aesthetic found in Christ. This sensibility and perceptive capability is encountered and formed in human communities who stand under the 'glory of the cross.'"[11] Any artwork used in the liturgy, and this would include a piece of literature used in a sermon, must be consonant with the "kenotic beauty" of the cross, and must form hearers to see the world more deeply according to the kenotic life of God in Christ so this can become their own way of life. This is the "propaganda" or separable message that must drive the sermon, the liturgy, and all art incorporated into them. Not all artwork meets this criterion.

While the differences between the purpose of art and that of sermons require the preacher to exercise caution in using literature in sermons, these differences also invite preachers to allow the purposes of artworks to influence their own preaching. The use of literature in sermons is one way the preacher can do this. Specifically, the comparison between art and preaching invites preachers, where possible, to make their sermons less like propaganda and more like art. Religious art is often second-rate precisely because it is concerned not with the integrity, goodness, and beauty of the artwork itself, but rather with conveying a certain message that precedes and drives the artwork. This danger befalls preaching as well, affecting both the rhetoric and the content of sermons.

In terms of the content of sermons, the preacher's desire to proclaim a predetermined message can lead her to gloss over the complexity and messiness of both the biblical text and life itself. Anna Carter Florence faults preachers for seeking to prematurely solve the challenges presented by biblical texts, warning that preachers tend to "tie [the text] to a chair and torture it" until it yields the meaning the preacher wants it to have, or came to it looking for.[12] Having this attitude toward the text, preachers are only looking for the "right" interpretation of the text rather than for what is possible in it. Likewise, because preachers are committed beforehand to the Good News as their core message, they may not sufficiently take account of the reality of the world itself. O'Connor criticizes Christian writers for this error: "The sorry religious novel comes about when the writer supposes that because of his belief, he is somehow dispensed from the obligation to penetrate concrete reality. He will think that the eyes of the Church or of the Bible or of his particular theology have already done the seeing for him, and that his business is to rearrange this essential vision into satisfying patterns, getting himself as little dirty in the process as possible."[13] Being a Christian artist, she argues, ought to propel one toward a deeper engagement with material reality and a willingness to portray its messiness, precisely to show grace and hence meaning in these aspects of life. As Jeremy Begbie states, "The artist cannot pass lightly over the disorder of the creation without being guilty of colossal self-deception and becoming utterly irrelevant to the needs of a broken and torn world."[14] Christian artists run the risk of solving these problems too quickly by falling back on received dogma rather than deeply wrestling with these issues themselves. This is a danger in sermons also—the risk that the preacher's prior commitment to the message of the Gospel might cause her not to really see the world, and thus to overlook or minimize the tragedy and evil in it.

Both in her approach to texts and to the world itself, the preacher would do well to adopt the artist's courageous perception of the world in order to be more convincing when she points to grace. As well as cultivating the artist's sensibility in her own words, the preacher can be helped in this endeavor by drawing on the words of other artists. The use of literature in sermons is one way to achieve this deeper engagement with reality and to push the sermon itself toward something more open-ended, less packaged. Literature can help preachers locate the real and the sacramental dimension of the real, because literature, as an art form, often states truths more boldly and honestly than we feel we can say them in sermons; there is a rawness to works of art that can open the sermon up to truth. The sermon becomes more about presenting the complexity of texts and life as we experience them rather than trying too quickly to solve or settle the mysteries of faith and life. Literature can help us do this, as it does not have a predetermined message but seeks to portray the world as the artist sees it. It is out of this encounter with the real, and a willingness to portray it in all its complexity and messiness, that the preacher gains credibility to show how this messy and complex world is still touched by grace, redeemed by God. While this latter aspect of the preacher's task may well not be shared by the artist, by making use of the artist's vision of the world, the preacher shows that she has reckoned with the world as it is, and thus has more authority to proclaim grace in the midst of this reality.

An example of how a piece of literature can open up the messiness of a biblical text (and of life itself) is found in Anna Akmatova's poem, "Lot's Wife."[15] In this poem she surprisingly offers a defense of Lot's wife's decision to look back at Sodom as she fled the city with her family: "a wild grief in his wife's bosom cried,/ *Look back, it is not too late for a last sight/Of the red towers of your native Sodom, the square/Where once you sang, the gardens you shall mourn....*" Akmatova transforms Lot's wife from an anonymous person who disregarded the angel's warning and made a foolish choice that cost her life, to a woman wracked by the tragedy of losing her home, such that in that tragedy she made a choice we can understand and sympathize with. This poem does not offer the standard theological interpretation of Lot's wife, in which she is usually portrayed as an example of disobedience or unreadiness to follow God. The use of this poem in a sermon would destabilize the effort to offer this predictable interpretation of her. However, this very destabilizing effect could be a gift to a sermon, complicating and enriching it—for instance, by illustrating the challenge of following God in faith when it might mean severing ourselves from all that we have known and loved. In this way poems present a text untamed, and we can use the unexpected or even scandalous insights of literature to deepen our appreciation of biblical texts, and to surprise ourselves by what we find in them. Using literature that offers an unorthodox perspective on biblical texts allows us to present the complexity and mystery of texts and of life itself without prematurely trying to tidy them up.

In terms of the style or rhetoric of sermons, the preacher would also do well to follow the example of artists and poets, in particular the criteria of O'Connor—that a piece of art needs to "be good in itself and work in itself," and needs to "carry its meaning inside it." The best sermons convey the Good News organically through the experience of the sermon itself, while the less skillful ones awkwardly attach a statement of meaning, usually to the end of the sermon, which has not emerged organically from the sermon itself. In this instance the sermon does not "work in itself," but has to be roped into the service of the Gospel that it does not of itself adequately proclaim.

One remedy for this tendency is for preachers to make their language and rhetoric more poetic. Poetry seeks to speak of mysteries that cannot be directly spoken, to speak at the edges of what words can say. When we get to the limits of what can be expressed, we turn to poetic language, which in its compactness, intensity, musicality, and suggestive power comes closest to expressing the inexpressible. Preaching, too, seeks to express the inexpressible—in fact, the most inexpressible mystery of all, which is the mystery of God and God's relationship to us. Thus it is natural that preaching uses the devices of poetry—imagery, rhythm, repetition, qualities of sound—in order to convey these truths. The preacher can use poetics in crafting her own words, but can also employ the words of poets to assist her efforts to speak at the edges of the sayable. A good poem communicates in this way. So the use of such a poem in a sermon can help the whole sermon communicate poetically, touching upon inexpressible mysteries and making them palpably present. Stylistically, the use of a poem in a sermon can move the sermon away from propaganda toward something more artful in which the meaning or message of the sermon is "carried inside it," conveyed by the style, rhetoric, and experience of the sermon itself rather than being boiled down into a statement that is separable from the experience of the sermon as a whole.

The nature and purpose of sermons is not always the same as those of literature, which means that caution is necessary when using literature in sermons. However, the nature and purpose of literature also commends its use in sermons, provided the preacher is aware of the challenges involved. Using literature in sermons can make the entire sermon more artful–more poein the second stanzqtic, more open to both reality and mystery, more able to proclaim the Good News in the midst of the messiness and complexity of both life and biblical texts.

In addition to these overarching considerations, there are also a few specific guidelines to keep in mind when using literature in sermons:

1. Literature is culturally embedded, so it is important to be sensitive about whether the piece of literature you plan to use in your sermon is accessible to the culture in which you are preaching. It is risky to assume that everyone in a given congregation will know any particular work of literature or even the identity of any given writer or poet. Make sure that your hearers are not left out of these references. Furthermore, a particular risk with longer works, such as novels, is that if you do not assume familiarity with the work, and have to explain the plot and characters at great length to make your use of the novel work in the sermon, this can make the use of the novel too cumbersome, burdening the sermon rather than enlivening it.

2. When telling a story from a literary work, be careful not to reveal details of the work that will spoil the story for those who have not yet read it.

3. As the poem "Lot's Wife" demonstrates, literature that comments on biblical texts inevitably offers an interpretation of those texts. Be mindful of what that interpretation is, and if it is not the same as your interpretation of the text, make sure that this piece of literature contributes to your interpretation rather than undermining it. As "Lot's Wife" indicates, a piece of literature can contribute to your sermon precisely by complicating it, but this only works if you acknowledge and work with the complexity or areas of disagreement with your own interpretation. To ignore the artist's interpretation is to invite discordance and confusion in your sermon.

4. Examples from literature and poetry as used in sermons have some similar qualities as other sermon illustrations, and thus some similar cautions apply. As with any illustration, it is important to ask if the poem or novel draws attention to the text or distracts from it. Likewise, it is important to ask if the illustration from literature supports the sermon as a whole or overshadows it. This is a particular danger with very powerful literary

examples, which like any effective illustration may be so potent that they are the only things the hearer remembers, rather than the message of the Gospel.

5. Related to this consideration, there is a danger in sermons of employing too many words of other people rather than your own words. A sermon peppered with quotes, whether from poems or other sources, undermines the authority and presence of the preacher. Your hearers really want to hear you more than they want to hear the words of others, no matter how lovely or insightful they may be. If you rely too much on other people's words, it gives the impression that you do not have as much to say about matters of importance as others do, or that you do not feel you have the authority to say it in your own words. Speaking in your own words is often more powerful than referring to others' words because it conveys that what you are saying truly comes from you and is what you personally believe and know. This authenticity is ultimately what converts hearers, more than hearing from experts and famous artists does. This guideline ought not to discourage preachers from using literature in sermons, but rather serve as a caution against relying too much on any other person's words to carry the weight of your preaching.

With these cautions in mind, we now turn to particular examples of how literature can contribute to sermons. In the following section, I explore ways that specific lectionary texts can be opened up through dialogue with poems that comment on these texts. In keeping with guideline 5 above, the best use of these poems in sermons would not be to supplant the preacher's own interpretation of the text but use them as a contrapuntal voice that can further and deepen what the preacher herself wants to say about the text.

Part II – Poems in Dialogue with Lectionary Texts

Genesis 22:1–18 (Year A, Proper 8)

This story, variously called the binding of Isaac, the sacrifice of Isaac, or the testing of Abraham, is certainly one of the most troubling passages in Hebrew scripture. For that very reason, it has attracted quite a bit of attention from writers and other artists who find grist for their creativity in the story's baffling and disturbing qualities. This passage is also one of the most difficult to preach in scripture: Not only does it portray God in a very troubling light, as one who would command that a parent kill his child, but it offers a disturbing model for human behavior in what Abraham does. Usually in sermons, we treat scriptural figures as moral examples for us to emulate, and certainly this would be our natural approach to interpreting the deeds of Abraham, the father of faith. However, it is highly problematic to argue that we should copy Abraham's behavior in this pericope in any straightforward sense. Soren Kierkegaard, in his work *Fear and Trembling*, bitterly mocks preachers who simplistically claim that we should follow

Abraham's example in this story and then are shocked when parents go home and kill their children.[16]

These difficulties in preaching this passage make it natural that we would turn to the wealth of literature on this text to assist our own interpretation of it. Emily Dickinson offers one particularly unsparing interpretation of the text, which lays the blame for the incident squarely at God's feet.[17] When God gave the command to slay Isaac, with "not a hesitation–/Abraham complied–," in response to which, "Flattered by obeisance–/Tyranny demurred–". Dickinson draws the following lesson from this interaction: "Moral–with a mastiff/Manners may prevail." God here is portrayed as a tyrant, or a dangerous and brutal animal (a "mastiff"), whom one must placate and flatter with obedience to get him to revoke his dreadful command. Like the Akmatova poem on Lot's wife, this Dickinson poem is an example of an artwork that declares what the poet sees in the text, unconstrained by any need to make the interpretation consonant with theological orthodoxy. Hence, to use this poem in a sermon is to open up the messiness of the text rather than trying to tidy it up or square it too easily with orthodoxy. The usefulness of doing this, of using this shocking, even blasphemous poem in a sermon, is that it names feelings many have about God's behavior in this text. Certainly it is reasonable to feel that God is a vicious and brutal tyrant in the demand he makes to Abraham. Since, as discussed earlier, preachers have a responsibility to preach this text as Good News, it is probably necessary to move beyond Dickinson's interpretation of this text, and particularly of God's action in it. However, to start with her interpretation could be useful, since it lays out quite natural and reasonable reactions that many have to this text.

One stimulating preaching strategy would be to compare Dickinson's view of God's relationship to humans in this text with that offered by Christopher Smart in his poem "Faith," in which the angelic voice that stops Abraham from killing his son says, "Know God is everlasting love,/ And must revoke such harsh commands." The preacher would still have to explain why it is that God, who is "everlasting love," would give the "harsh command" in the first place. The preacher could also wrestle with Smart's concluding exhortation: "Then let us imitate the Seer, /And tender with complaint grace/Ourselves, our souls and children here,/Hereafter in a better place." The necessity for absolute faith in God, and even the willingness to offer to God those parts of our lives that are most precious to us, may well be the message the preacher wishes to draw from this text. However, the counterpoint of this poem with the Dickinson poem warns the preacher away from offering this interpretation too easily.

Yet another fascinating interpretation of this text is found in Wilfred Owen's "The Parable of the Old Man and the Young," in which Abraham's willingness to sacrifice his son is taken as a metaphor for men's willingness to sacrifice their sons in wars. Abraham not only binds his son on the altar, but does so "with belts and straps," and moreover "builded parapets and trenches there." When the angel of God demands that Abraham desist from killing his son and that he offer "the Ram of Pride" instead of his own child to God, Abraham disregards this command of sanity and compassion and continues with his planned slaughter: "But the old man would not so, but slew his son,/And half the see of Europe, one by one." For Owen, this scripture text becomes a vehicle for condemning war in general and World War I in particular. But it could also be used in a sermon to question our own willingness to engage in violence, supposing it to be God's will. In contrast to Dickinson, who holds Abraham innocent in this story, Owen sees God as the innocent party, who pleads for restraint, and it is Abraham who is culpably bloodthirsty.

2. Genesis 32:22–32 (Year A, Proper 13)

Denise Levertov's "Where is the Angel" and Gerard Manley Hopkins' "Carrion Comfort" are two poems that engage the story of Jacob wrestling with the angel. In "Carrion Comfort," Hopkins experiences God fighting against him fiercely, even mercilessly: "O thou terrible, why wouldst thou rude on me/Thy wring-world right foot rock? lay a lionlimb against me? scan/ With darksome devouring eyes my bruised bones?" The answer Hopkins gives is "That my chaff might fly; my grain lie, sheer and clear." This wrestling, even though it brings him to the brink of despair, is purifying. His syntax also captures the confusing tangle of God and Jacob that is evident in the biblical text, in which the pronoun "he" is repeatedly used to the point that it is not always easy to tell whether Jacob or the angel is being referred to. Hopkins conveys this tangle in the final lines of the poem: "Cheer whom though? The hero whose heaven-handling flung me, foot trod/Me? or me that fought him? O which one? is it each one?" God and Jacob cannot be easily disentangled in this struggle, nor is it clear which of them defeated the other in this wrestling match. The only thing that can be said for certain is that in the end, the human wrestler recognizes that he has been fighting with God: "I wretch lay wrestling with (my God!) my God." This recognition, in the midst of a painful, frightening, and even life-threatening struggle, is finally the blessing accorded to Hopkins, as it was to Jacob.

By contrast, Denise Levertov's "Where is the Angel" portrays the situation of one who is bereft because of the absence of this divine wrestling companion. Without this angel, the poet breathes a "tepid air" and lives in a "gentle haze," where her feelings are dulled. Most serious of all, in her heart it is "pleasant," but "when I open/my mouth to speak, I too/ am soundless." The vague, muffled state in which she is living has silenced her poetic voice. Thus she cries out for the angel who will break through this complacent torpor and free her voice: "Where is the angel/to wrestle with me and wound/not my thigh but my throat,/so curses and blessings flow storming out/and the glass shatters, and the iron sunders?"

This poem forms a stimulating counterpoint to the Hopkins poem on the subject of our differing experiences of relationship with God. While the experience of struggle and wrestling with God may well be frightening and overwhelming, it may be worse to feel distant and disconnected from God, as Levertov is. While Hopkins feels his very life imperiled by God's powerful nearness, at the end of the poem the epiphany for which he longs occurs, as well as the purification that he acknowledges is necessary. For Levertov, by contrast, the soul is stagnant and creativity is stultified in the pleasant but deadly absence of God. These two poets could illustrate two phases of our relationship with God, tending toward the conclusion that we might pray for God's terrifying nearness and the wrestling that ensues, rather than being satisfied with a distant God.

3. Psalm 42 (Year C, Proper 7), Psalm 54 (Year B, Proper 20), Psalm 79 (Year C, Proper 20), Psalm 80 (Year A, Advent 4 and Proper 22; Year B, Advent 1; Year C, Advent 4 and Proper 20), and Other Lament Psalms

Gerard Manley Hopkins' poem, "Thou art indeed just, Lord, if I contend," and George Herbert's poem "The Flower" are not explicitly linked to these particular psalms, but both poems exhibit qualities of a lament, which makes for a fruitful pairing with these and other lament psalms. The Hopkins poem begins with a quote from Jeremiah 12:1 and following (a text not found in the Revised Common Lectionary), and since Jeremiah 12 takes the form of an individual lament, it makes sense that the Hopkins poem would parallel the lament form in certain respects. The form of the individual lament psalm contains certain common elements: It begins with an invocation, an initial plea to God for help, followed by a complaint, describing the speaker's sufferings. Then follows the demand, what the speaker wants God to do. There is often a condemnation of enemies, an affirmation of confidence in God because of God's deeds in the past, a confession of sins, and usually an acknowledgment of divine response, followed by praise of God or the promise to praise God.

The Hopkins and Herbert poems seem almost to divide the lament form in half. Hopkins speaks from the middle of the experience of suffering and calls out to God for help *in extremis*, while Herbert speaks from a position of well-being after having being delivered from suffering. In the poem Herbert looks back in retrospect and describes the desperate situation in which Hopkins currently finds himself. Hopkins cries out to God, "Wert thou my enemy, O thou my friend,/How wouldst thou worse, I wonder, than thou dost/ Defeat, thwart me?" This cry echoes the outrage in many psalms, which take God to task for treating poorly those who have sworn fidelity to God, those who are God's own people (see, for instance, Ps.

44:17–19). Hopkins also feels aggrieved that "sinners' ways prosper," while, by contrast "disappointment all I endeavor end[s]," just as the psalmist often wonders why the enemies of God thrive and are victorious, while God's own people suffer defeat and humiliation. Hopkins then turns his attention to the lushness of the natural world on which God's blessing seems so bountiful: "See, banks and brakes/Now, leaved how thick! laced they are again/with fretty chervil, look, and fresh winds shakes/Them." God's renewal has come again to these natural places, with a resurgence of industry and productivity, for "birds build." In the midst of this fecundity he alone is sterile and unproductive: "but not I build; no, but strain,/ Time's eunuch, and not breed one work that wakes." Hopkins' complaint about the seemingly arbitrary and fickle way in which God nurtures some and starves others parallels the psalmist's complaint that God, who "brought a vine out of Egypt ... drove out the nations and planted it," so that "it took deep root and filled the land," now has broken down the walls of the vineyard, "so that all who pass along the way pluck its fruit" (Ps. 80:8, 9, 12). Hopkins' poem ends halfway through the typical lament form with the anguished plea, "Mine, O thou lord of life, send my roots rain."

To such a powerful plea and accusation it is important to have some kind of answer in a sermon, and Herbert's "The Flower" provides it. Herbert speaks after he has been delivered from a situation that sounds not unlike Hopkins'. Indeed, Herbert speaks in a kind of wonder that he was somehow saved: "Who would have thought my shriveled heart/Could have recovered greenness? It was gone/Quite underground." Just as Hopkins feels barren when viewing the lush greenery of spring, so too Herbert experienced a withering of his "greenness." As Hopkins pled for a revival of growth and fertility, so Herbert marvels that this renewal has happened to him: "How fresh, O Lord, how sweet and clean/Are thy returns! even as the flowers in spring." As Hopkins begs to be given again the power to create, so Herbert exults that "After so many deaths I live and write." Both poems are at their core about the experience of creativity—the anguish when it feels impossible to write, and the joy when words begin to flow again.

Herbert, perhaps because he has emerged from the depths of suffering in which Hopkins still languishes, offers a perspective on why such suffering occurs. Herbert describes his earlier state, in which he grew upward like a flower, "as if heaven were mine own." God smote him down because of this pride, and his afflictions were in order to "make us see we are but flowers that glide." Herbert closes with a caution: "Who would be more,/Swelling through store,/Forfeit their Paradise by their pride." His interpretation of the afflictions and barrenness through which he lived is that it was a necessary lesson to cure him of pride, of thinking he is of more substance than a mere flower. This realization parallels the confession of sins that is often part of the psalm of lament; having blamed God and blamed enemies, the psalmist finally turns inward to contemplate how his own sinfulness may have brought him into his current suffering. The Herbert poem also contains the latter portions of the lament psalm in which the psalmist, having become assured of God's help, offers praise to God.

Like the psalms of lament, both of these poems are brimming with insights into the human condition, and thus make rich material for sermons on suffering, God's providence, or the mysteries of election and vocation. The Hopkins poem as a whole speaks eloquently to the outrage that people of faith feel when, having devoted themselves to God wholeheartedly, they experience unmerited suffering. For Hopkins, the sting in his suffering is that the work that he wants to awaken is work that he believes God has called him to. This experience is not unique to poets; it can affect anyone who feels stymied in their expression of their vocation, and questions whether God has called them in order to mock them, or whether they mistook God's call in the first place. These kinds of obstacles can lead to profound doubt in the goodness of God. When around them people of faith see other people thriving who do not seem to live according to God's ways, or when they see nature flourishing in all its bounty while they are deprived of any sustenance, it can lead to a sense of despair that Hopkins captures vividly in this poem of lament. A preacher can and must acknowledge these experiences of suffering, these moments when God seems more like an enemy than a friend. At the same time, the preacher can gently offer the insights found in Herbert's poem, which suggest that sometimes we feel thwarted in our lives and work because we need to learn a deeper dependence on God, a deeper sense of God's power. Our pride in our own achievements may need to be tempered by the realization that our fruitfulness depends on God and must be centered in God. These two poems together offer rich resources for pondering these aspects of the human condition.

Part III – Resources for a Sermon Series on Creation

The story of God's creation of the world (Gen. 1:1–2:25) is found in various places in the lectionary, but not all in one sequence. Portions are read on the Feast of the Baptism of Our Lord, Trinity Sunday, and a few of the Propers in ordinary time. Partly because these texts are broken up and scattered throughout the lectionary, it is rare in preaching that the story of God's creation of the world gets the sustained attention it deserves. Poets and writers, however, give a great deal of attention to this story; this is in part because, since writers are themselves creators, they are drawn to exploring the nature of God's creativity. A rich sermon series could be developed that makes use of this wealth of poetic treatments of these texts. The series could touch upon a variety of important theological topics, such as the nature of God as Creator (why and how God creates the world), the nature of that which God has created (including humankind), and the importance of our human stewardship of creation. Although in this series I have not specifically addressed the Fall (Gen. 3), any consideration of the human relationship to creation must reckon with the depth of human sin and the consequences of that sin. We now live in a time of ecological crisis in which we are facing a reckoning for the ways in which human activity has compromised God's good creation to an alarming extent. There is an urgent need for us humans to reconnect with the wonder of God's good creation and our role as stewards of it. Nowhere is this wonder and responsibility more clearly set forth than in the Genesis creation account, so this makes these texts a rich and necessary resource for preaching.

Sermon #1: Why Did God Create the World?

James Weldon Johnson's glorious poem "The Creation," from *God's Trombones,* offers a vivid account of God's creation of the world, beginning by tackling the core theological question, "Why did God create the world?" Johnson gives his answer to this question in the opening lines of the poem: "And God stepped out into space,/And he looked around and said:/ I'm lonely– /I'll make me a world."[18] This statement raises the interesting question of whether God *needed* to create the world in order to fulfill a need in Godself, which according to many theologians would violate the principle that God is complete in Godself, not needing anything outside of God to fulfill God's wholeness. According to this account, God created out of a sheer superabundance of love; the love that defines the Trinitarian relations in the Godhead simply spilled over to create the world. This is not the picture we see in Johnson's poem, where God seems to need creation and, ultimately, finds God's loneliness healed only when he creates humankind. A preacher could do something interesting with this contrast between Johnson's depiction of God and the classical theological position. What if we entertained the possibility that God really does need us? What if we considered that, as beautiful as all of creation is, there is something unique about the relationship between God and humankind that alone satisfies not only a need in us but also in God? Might this understanding of our role in creation inspire us to recommit ourselves to our primary relationship to the God who is lonely without us?

Sermon #2: How Did God Create the World?

In addition to addressing the question of *why* God created the world, in "The Creation" Johnson also vividly portrays *how* God does it. In this poem the creator God is portrayed wonderfully anthropomorphically as a being who is not at all afraid to get his hands dirty and whose creativity is very tangible, very gritty. God's smile causes the light to break forth, but then "God reached out and took the light in his hands,/And God rolled the light around in his hands/Until he made the sun." God similarly creates valleys and mountains by walking across the earth and making footprints. He spits out the seven seas, claps his eyes and thunder rolls, and waves his hand to create the animals. It is when God creates humankind that he becomes the most physically involved: he "scoops the clay" from the river, then kneels down, and "Like a mammy bending over her baby,/Kneeled down in the dust/Toiling over a lump of clay/Till he shaped it in his own image." Johnson marvels that the God who "lit the sun…flung the stars…rounded the earth in the middle of his hand" would bend down so intimately and laboriously to create humans. In this way Johnson spans the stately, imperial creation account in Genesis 1 with the more intimate, folksy, anthropomorphic portrayal of the creation of humankind in Genesis 2:4b–7. This span gives the preacher an opportunity to talk about the differences between these two accounts, and what each one tells us about who God is, what creation is, and who we humans are in relationship to both.

A lovely counterpoint to Johnson's creation account is offered in *The Magician's Nephew*, a volume in C. S. Lewis' *Chronicles of Narnia*. Lewis portrays the lion Aslan (the Christ-figure in the Narnia books) creating through his voice, a marvelous series of events witnessed by visitors to Narnia from our world. When the voice begins to sing, it seems to come from all directions at once and even from the earth itself. It is the most beautiful sound ever heard. When the voice begins, all is dark and cold and empty, but then two marvels happen at the same time:

> One was that the voice was suddenly joined by other voices; more voices than you could possibly count. They were in harmony with it, but far higher up the scale: cold, tingling, silvery voices. The second wonder was that the blackness overhead, all at once, was blazing with stars .... The new stars and the new voices began at exactly the same time…it was the stars themselves who were singing, and it was the First Voice, the deep one, which had made them appear and made them sing.[19]

The Voice continues to sing, and as it varies its tune, sun, moon, trees, plants, and animals all appear. (Interestingly, in this account God/Aslan does not create humankind, for the humans come from our world).

This creation account is not as visceral as Johnson's (in Narnia God does not get his hands, or paws, dirty), but Lewis, like Johnson, conveys in a beautiful way how God takes thought to each creature being created, creates them in a way unique to their own character and purpose, and takes evident delight in creating them. Both versions depict the beauty of the world's creation in a way that is both moving and delightful–among other things calling us to a renewed care of the earth that God has so lovingly created.

Sermon #3: What Did God Create? Praising God for Creation

After discussing the various interpretations of how God created the world, the next natural step is to marvel at all that God created and to praise God for it. Poets and other writers offer effusive praise for all that God created, even as they wonder at the opulence and complexity of it all. "Glory be to God for dappled things," Gerard Manley Hopkins exults in "Pied Beauty": "for skies of couple-colour as a brinded cow;/for rose-moles all in stipple upon trout that swim." He marvels at the paradox that all this variety—"all things counter, original, spare, strange"—were created by the one "whose beauty is past change." The God who is unchanging nevertheless set in motion a universe of constant change and dazzling diversity. All Hopkins can conclude from this abundant miracle is the necessity to "Praise Him." Thomas Traherne, in his "Meditation on the Six Days of Creation," describes how at the creation Earth "spring[s] from her bed, gay, vigorous, and sound:/Her face ten thousand beauties now adorn, /With blessings numberless from plenty's horn." Given all this bounty, Traherne chides "wretched man" if "he forget to praise that liberal hand,/ Out-spread from sea to sea, from land to land." The beauty of creation, in both these poems and in many others, such as Richard Wilbur's "Praise in Summer" and Andrew Marvell's "the Garden," issues an insistent call for humans to praise the one who created all that we see, enjoy, and rely upon for our life's continuance. The preacher could use these poems to reinforce the obligation and joy of praising God for the wonders of creation, perhaps employing these poems to buttress the repeated calls of the psalmist to praise God for all the bounty of the created world.

To complicate this picture, and to ponder some of the ambiguities of our created existence, the preacher could draw on William Blake's "The Tyger." Here Blake considers the most awesome of animals, the tiger, "burning bright/In the forests of the night," and asks, "What immortal hand or eye/ Could frame thy fearful symmetry?" Blake reasons that only a fearsome Creator could have created such a terrifying beast. Considering the tiger's ferocious body and brain, Blake asks, "what dread grasp/Dare its deadly terrors grasp?" Blake wonders how the Creator felt when he finished making this dread creature: "Did he smile his work to see?/ Did he who made the Lamb make thee?" This poignant question raises a host of theological questions: How is it that the world, so full of beauty and abundance, is also full of perils and their attendant suffering? Why did God create a world with creatures like the tiger, that could easily kill the human beings made in God's image? Why did God create a world containing earthquakes, volcanoes, and tornadoes? Why did God create a world in which suffering is inevitable? There is an added poignancy to the question in relation to the tiger, since in our day, in contrast to Blake's time, the power relationship between the human and the tiger has dramatically shifted in favor of the human. Tigers are now a critically endangered species, driven to the brink of extinction by human activities such as hunting and the destruction of the tiger's habitat. One might more easily shift the theological question raised by this poem to ask why God created humankind with its propensity to destroy the lives of God's other creatures, including the tiger, as well as God's creation itself. Perhaps it is more accurate at this point in the story of our beleaguered planet to say that we humans (instead of tigers) are the ones who are dreadful and dangerous in relation to the rest of God's creation. The preacher would have to be exceedingly careful making this argument, but if done well, such a proposal could call congregations to repentance, and a new way of relating to God's creation and the creatures in it.

Sermon #4: The Creation of Humankind

The mystery and marvel of the human being has been a source of much creative work on the part of poets and other writers. The combination of grandeur and vulnerability, goodness and sin, capacity for happiness and for misery, astonishing gifts and equally astonishing pettiness, have fascinated writers over the centuries, provoking them to wonder why God created us with this strange mixture of traits. George Herbert's "The Pulley" and "Man" comment in particularly thought-provoking ways on the ambiguity of the human condition as God created it.

In "The Pulley," Herbert depicts God showering all manner of blessings on humans in creating them; but then, when almost all the blessings were distributed, God decides not to give rest to his creature. God realizes that if he should bestow rest on the human, "He would adore my gifts instead of me,/ And rest in Nature, not the God of Nature,/so both should losers be." Thus God decides to let his human creation keep all the other blessings, but keep them "with repining restlessness," so that "If goodness lead him not, yet weariness/May toss him to my breast." Herbert proposes that the fundamental lack of rest within the human soul was placed there by God when we were created for the very purpose of driving us to God, where we ultimately belong. This poem states in its own way St. Augustine's statement that God has made us for Godself, and our hearts are restless until they rest in God. There is much rich food for preaching in the idea that our very dissatisfaction—the impossibility of finding fulfillment of our desires despite all the gifts we have been given—is a sign of our fundamental orientation toward God.

In "Man" Herbert similarly meditates on what our created state tells us about our relationship to God. He opens the poem by commenting that "I heard this day/That none doth build a stately habitation,/But he that means to dwell therein." If that is so, "What house more stately hath there been,/ Or can be, than is Man?" The bulk of the poem is Herbert's description of the grandeur and "stateliness" of the human being, who is more fruitful than trees, who has reason and speech as animals do not, and who is crafted with beautiful symmetry. Moreover, all creation serves humans: "For us the winds do blow,/The earth doth rest, heavens move, and fountains flow./ Nothing we see but means our good,/As our delight or as our treasure." Here Herbert echoes Genesis 1:26–30 in which God declares that God's creation is full of gifts to assist in human flourishing. If the human is herself beautiful and marvelous, and if creation serves our good in so many ways, surely this means that we are the "stately habitation" God has built in order to dwell therein. Thus Herbert concludes his poem and rests his case: "Since then, my God, thou hast/So brave a palace built, O dwell in it,/That it may dwell with thee at last!" As in "The Pulley," Herbert here too meditates on the ambiguity of the human condition; as marvelously made as we are, and as wondrously placed in a good and accommodating creation, we are still essentially an empty house, no matter how stately and "brave," until God chooses to dwell in us.

"Man" raises several theological issues for the preacher to address. Like "The Pulley," the poem dramatizes our grandeur as humans and our need for God. "Man" goes farther than "The Pulley" in describing the glories of human nature and existence, which the preacher can use to call hearers to the praise of God and also to good stewardship of the gifts we have been given. Unlike "The Tyger," both "Man" and "The Pulley" portray the world as beneficent for humans, a contrast that offers grist for the preacher in tackling the issue of the fundamental goodness of creation, despite the natural evils that are part of it. Both of these Herbert poems ultimately call us to recognize our dependence on God, call us to prayer for God's presence, and point Christians to Christ as the answer to Herbert's prayer that the God who created us would redeem and fulfill that creation by coming to dwell with us in Jesus of Nazareth.

9

The Living Afterlife of a Dead Prophet: Words That Keep Speaking

BY WALTER BRUEGGEMANN

John Holbert, happily, is alive and well. He is getting old, but he is not dead. The discussion that follows concerns a dead prophet, one who stays alive even in his death.

I.

Elisha had a vigorous ministry, both public and pastoral. It concludes, according to the biblical text, with his instigation of a political coup in 2 Kings 9:1. After that we hear no more from him except for his odd encounter with King Joash (2 Kings 13:14–19) and the even more curious note of 2 Kings 13:20–21 that is the subject of this discussion. In these two terse final verses (usually ignored by the commentaries), it is reported:

- that Elisha died and was buried;
- that another man was being buried later;
- that due to pressure from a "marauding band" (presumably of Moabites), the second dead man was thrown into Elisha's grave.

We are not told why that action was taken; perhaps it was to protect the corpse from abuse at the hands of thugs. In any case,

123

- When the corpse "touched the bones of Elisha," he was restored to life.

This report is readily slotted as an "anecdote" to go along with much of the Elisha narrative that is "legend." One must, nevertheless, wonder why the narrative is there. My assumption, and the basis for what follows in this discussion, is that the "miracle of resurrection" enacted by contact with the bones of the dead prophet is to indicate that the prophet still has continuing effective power for life, even after he is dead. That is, his body is "radioactive" and continues to emit energy for life even dead, the kind of active energy evident in the report of Jesus who was "immediately aware that power had gone forth from him" (Mark 5:30; Luke 8:46). This report on Elisha has set me to thinking, in the context of John Holbert's work, of the durable life-giving force of prophetic word and act. I wish to develop that thought in two directions concerning two primary genres of prophetic speech, the kind that "prophetic preaching" engages in only carefully and gingerly.

II.

The primary genre of prophetic speech in the eighth to seventh century B.C.E. is the "speech of judgment" that consists in an *indictment* for actions of failed obedience and a *sentence* that states the God-given judgment on the basis of the indictment.[1] The speech of judgment derives from and is based on the old covenant rhetoric of *commandment* and *sanction (blessing* or *curse)*. (It is because of common ignorance about the structure of covenant faith that prophetic speeches of judgment are nearly impossible in the contemporary church).

From among the many prophetic speeches of judgment, I here focus on an oracle of Jeremiah offered twice in the text. In Jeremiah 6:13–15, the speech of judgment is voiced as *indictment* (vv. 13–15a) and *sentence* (v. 15b). (See the same words in 8:10–12 where the elements of the speech are inverted.) The indictment in the poem traces self-serving leadership (v. 13) followed by false assurances of *shalom* (v. 14), leading to a verdict of "shamelessness" without being "ashamed," no longer having a capacity to blush in embarrassment. The poem characterizes a people so morally numb or cynical that it is no longer embarrassed about its deep moral failure. The sentence, introduced with a characteristic "therefore," anticipates "fall, punishment, overthrow."

Here I focus on that inability to feel shame because our moral sensibility has been overcome by aggressive greed sustained by deception. The focus on "shame" goes beneath guilt and juridical categories to the most intimate measure of social sensibility.[2] There is no doubt that Jeremiah spoke this poetry at a time and place in the political-military crisis of Jerusalem that he re-imagines as a moral crisis—that is, the inability to discern public reality with reference to the covenantal expectations of YHWH. That much is uncontested in critical study.

With reference to the radioactive bones of Elisha, I propose we may go beyond critical questions to see that the poetic speech of the prophet (twice remembered in chapters 6 and 8) continues to have a life well beyond the immediate context. The ancient words, like the ancient bones, continue with vitality in subsequent social remembering and reflection concerning subsequent moral insensitivity. I can think of three instances in which "they do not know how to blush" continues to be a vital utterance in a community of moral reflection:

- In his great Stanford lectures, Abraham Heschel cites "a sense of ultimate embarrassment" as the ground for praise:

  Religion depends on what man does with his ultimate embarrassment. It is the awareness that the world is too great for him, the awareness of the grandeur and mystery of being, the awareness of being present at the unfolding of an inconceivable eternal saga. Embarrassment is the awareness of a incongruity of character and challenge, of perceptivity and reality, of knowledge and understanding, of mystery and comprehension.... It is a protection against...arrogance, hubris, self-deification. The end of embarrassment would be the end of humanity.[3]

- In the "McCarthy hearings," when Senator Joseph McCarthy was near the end of his nefarious career, the pixie-like attorney, Joseph Welch, asked him before the cameras, "Senator, have you at long last no shame?" Clearly the answer was, "No, no shame."
- Mayor Richard J. Daly (Chicago), caught in a profound political scandal, was asked at a press conference if he was embarrassed to be caught. His answer was, "Nothing embarrasses us."

I submit that the ancient utterance of Jeremiah keeps ringing in our ears, keeps offering vitality to evoke sensibility. We keep reading and pondering old texts, now in a context of napalm or torture in order to face the moral numbness of our culture. Perhaps Heschel, Welch, and Daly could have said all of this without the antecedent poetry of Jeremiah. But I doubt it. The words live and wait to be uttered and heard always again. In his "moral history of the twentieth century," Jonathan Glover writes of the "Residue of Moral Identity; Embarrassment." He takes up the hard case of the Nazi death camps and observes that they were kept hidden:

  It was fear of embarrassment, together with the fear of a public outcry, which led to policies of concealment .... Hitler and his circle did not like to be exposed to what their policies did to people. Even they could be embarrassed .... Even the top Nazis could feel the pressure of social disapproval. Perhaps even the top Nazis sometimes felt awkwardness, linked to the residue of an older moral identity. They tried to conceal the murder of the Jews.[4]

We may follow the judgment of Erik Erikson that shame is an elemental human awareness. The remarkable realization is that "shame" can be eradicated by sufficient moral callousness. But prophetic utterance makes that elemental awareness palpably available even in contexts where it has been forfeited. It is the hope of such utterance that the old bones and the old words can "live again."[5]

III.

The second genre of prophetic utterance is the oracle of promise that is richly offered in the sixth century, in the midst of exilic displacement.[6] Paul Hanson, in the wake of Gerhard Von Rad, has summarized the way in which Israelite religion engaged in "reapplication" of older tradition to turn old memories to new interpretive possibility.[7] In a season of hopelessness, the poets grounded hope in the promissory utterances of YHWH.

Here I focus on only one text, the lyrical promise of Isaiah 65:17–25 concerning a new heaven, a new earth, and a new Jerusalem. What strikes one about this most extreme and sweeping promise in the Old Testament is that it focuses on real human socioeconomic issues for a time to come: infant mortality (v. 20), protection of private property (vv. 21–22), childbirth (v. 23), and the environment (v. 25). The poem is, moreover, a lyrical utterance of possibility that the world has long since declared to be impossible. There can be little doubt of the historical location of this utterance, and scholars are generally agreed about a post-exilic venue for this lyrical articulation among Jewish poets who refused despair.

But of course the poetry would not stay still in that ancient context. Like the living bones, this lyrical poetry has kept surging toward new possibility in seasons of great disappointment and despair. As we are all aware, the New Testament utterance with a reflection on this poetry is the large anticipation of the church when Christ becomes all in all:

> Then I saw a new heaven and a new earth; for the first heaven and first earth had passed away, and the sea was no more. And I saw the holy city, the New Jerusalem, coming down out of heaven from God, prepared as a bride adorned for her husband. And I heard a loud voice from the throne saying,

> See, the home of God is among mortals.
>   He will dwell with them;
> They will be his peoples,
> And God himself will be with them;
>   he will wipe away every tear from their eyes.

Death will be no more;
Mourning and crying and pain will be no more,
For the first things have passed away.
And the one who was seated on the throne said, "See, I am making
all things new." (Rev. 21:1–5a)

Surely it is clear that the capacity of John to offer such a vision is based in the old poetry that continues in evocative vitality. It was, moreover, that ancient lyric that invited Christians under assault to trust in God's sure future and not give in to the brutal present tense. But of course the poetry pushes out beyond the canon. Perhaps the most distinctive generativity from that poem of Isaiah (or that sort of poem) is the great Washington, D.C., speech of Martin Luther King, Jr., "I have a Dream." The "dream" is indeed a God-given vision of what God will yet give that the world judges impossible. Like ancient Isaiah, King had no idea about how to get from here to there. But the poem, on credible lips, does its own work and generates its own future, in this case not least the great Civil Rights Acts that followed.

King stands in a long line of echoes from ancient Isaiah:

I have a dream that one day on the red hills of Georgia the sons of
former slaves and sons of former slave owners will be able to sit
down together at the table of brotherhood.
I have a dream that one day even the state of Mississippi, a desert
that swelters with the heat of injustice and oppression, will be
transformed into an oasis of freedom and justice.
I have a dream that my four little children will one day live in a
nation where they will not be judged by the color of their skin
but by the content of their character.
I have a dream today…
Let freedom ring from the snowcapped Rockies of Colorado!
Let freedom ring from the curvaceous peaks of California!
But not only that; let freedom ring from Stone Mountain of Georgia!
Lee freedom ring from Lookout Mountain of Tennessee!
Let freedom ring from every hill and molehill of Mississippi.
  From every mountainside, let freedom ring.[8]

There is no doubt that King's echoing speech invited (and continues to invite) his listeners out beyond present circumstance to new historical capabilities. The cadences of that speech, moreover, continue to evoke, empower, and energize. It is no wonder that Bruce Feiler can hear King's speech as a reiteration of all the great utterances of the U.S. drama of freedom:

His talk wove together many of the iconic themes from the 350-year
merger of the Hebrew Bible and America. He evokes the Pilgrims:

"Land where my fathers died, land of the Pilgrims' pride." He paid tribute to Lincoln and his use of Psalm 90: "Five score years ago, a great American, in whose symbolic shadow we stand together, signed the Emancipation Proclamation.".... In what is arguably the most famous speech by an American since the Gettysburg Address, Martin Luther King fused together Jefferson and Lincoln, Pilgrim and slave, Emma Lazarus and the Old State House bell, to set up his defining message from that "Old Negro spiritual" that Zora Neale Hurston had put into the mouths of the Israelites as they set out for the Promised land: "Free at last! Free at last! Thank God Almighty, we are free at last!"[9]

And the beat goes on!

IV.

My thought in this exposition is that prophetic preaching, as we undertake that task, is not only a momentary act of courage, though it is that. Much more, it is enlistment in cadences speech that reach back to Jeremiah and Isaiah, that travel with Heschel and Welch and King, and that alight for an instant in our own time and place. This practice of utterance is not unlike the bones of Elisha. Any preacher may hope to stumble into the grave of Elisha or into the cadences of Jeremiah and Isaiah. On many days we stumble in and come to the lively bones but are not activated, because often we are in denial or in despair; we are at the edge of silence; or we are too timed to speak. But then the old words energize, and we dare speak again, because the old words on our lips are live words, crafted afresh so that they become our own words of truth-telling.

Prophetic passages that appear in the lectionary are ordinarily treated in rather ad hoc fashion and are fairly sparse in usage and in the lectionary. But consider these texts when they are carriers of radioactive energy in a way that has vitality.

Amos 7:7–14 (Year B, Proper 10). This text features a confrontation between prophetic utterance that anticipates social dislocation and the established authority of the priest of the sanctuary who seeks to silence, because such truth-telling is more than can be borne. The text narrates the interaction of a daring risk of truth-telling and a society that resists such truth. The text invites the bold preacher to wonder what truth can be said, what truth needs to be heard in "the establishment," and what the costs of such truth-telling might be. There is no doubt that the regime of Jeroboam had created such a "bubble" of misperception that the truth sounded strange, even as it does now when uttered on our contemporary bubble of self-deception. Every truth-teller comes in the wake of Amos who declared that the establishment is penultimate and will be displaced.

Micah 5:2–5a (Year C, Fourth Sunday of Advent) voices a prophetic hope and a prophetic longing. It addresses little Bethlehem, the vulnerable village that is pitted not only against the Jerusalem establishment that Micah critiqued, but against the coming onslaught of Assyria. Bethlehem, of course, is the birthplace of David, and so the poem links the village to the great promises of the Davidic house that issued in messianism. The poem anticipates a new David who will come and act as the great shepherd-king who will assure peace to the villages, even in the face of the empire. The poem is drawn in Christian usage toward the birth and ministry of Jesus. Beyond that, however, is the prophetic conviction that God raises up human agents who can turn the course of history, even in the face of deep, brutal power. When all else fails for the vulnerable villagers, the prophets fall back to poetic hope that refuses to give in to the circumstance on the ground.

Zephaniah 3:14–20 (Year C, Third Sunday of Advent). The poem is a summons to Jerusalem—that is, to all Israel—to sing and dance and celebrate, because the "real king," YHWH, is coming among the dislocated, even in a situation of enormous social, political stress. It is anticipated that this new rule of God, after a spasm of imperial abuse, will reverse the course of history and cause well-being for Jerusalem. The coming intrusion of God will "give victory," "renew you," "remove disaster," "deal with your oppressors," and "gather the lame and outcast." All of that is summed up in the final phrase of the poem, "restore your fortunes." That phrase is used repeatedly for the end of exile and the wondrous homecoming of displaced people. The poem imagines the "direct rule" of YHWH, though clearly the poet anticipates a human agent who will do this work, even if that agent remains unnamed. Christians, as always, draw such expectation toward the coming of Jesus who will banish all causes of fearfulness in the world of those addressed. But, of course, prophetic hope makes an even more elemental claim, namely, that the public process of history is not a closed system that can sustain itself forever. The upshot of that claim is that every empire (including the Assyrian empire that Micah faced) is penultimate and will pass away. It is easy to succumb to the propaganda of the dominant system and imagine that present arrangements are permanent and beyond challenge. But prophetic faith is about God-given futures that do not derive from the present system but are a new gift. It is no wonder that the ones who heard the poem might rejoice, the way the lame and outcast did in the presence of Jesus.

Isaiah 35:4–7 (Year B, Proper 18). This promissory lyric anticipates a wondrous homecoming for all those who have not the power themselves to come home. The context is "forced migration" (exile), and the poet can see an end to such dislocation. The new presence of God in the midst of the vulnerable eradicates fear and provides energy for travel and song. The invitation is for the blind, the deaf, the lame, all those who lack clout in the old world. Beyond the vulnerable, moreover, the poem also envisions a recovery of the water supply for the animal world; one can imagine all of the animals gathering for a slow, cool long drink–a sign that the new creation of God has come in quite concrete ways. The new hope of the poem is that things will not stay as they have been, with fear, alienation, and deprivation. The urging of the poem is to be on the way to the new world that is breaking open by the power of God.

Isaiah 50:4–9 (Year B, Proper 19). The speaker of this poem reflects on the teaching vocation that is to instruct God's people in the demanding ways of faith. Such teaching, then as now, evoked resistance and hostility. In the face of such adversity, the teacher names the name of God…four times! Indeed, every unit of the poem begins with the divine name upon which the speaker relies. As a consequence of that divine reality, the teacher is confident about the truth-telling entrusted to him. In anticipation of Paul's argument about "justification," the speaker is confident that God "helps," so that no adversary can in fact harm him. The poem boldly imagines that the enemies will "wear out" and be "eaten up." The outcome is a word of reassurance for the hard ministry of prophetic instruction that goes against the grain of common expectation. But the teacher also recognizes that there is no alternative. This is the truth of the matter, and it must be faced.

V.

I am not sure a sermon series on texts like these can be sustained in most conventional Christian congregations. But we have to keep trying and exploring and experimenting. Were I to try that, it would be a series on how *evangelical truth* meets our *denial* and how *evangelical hope* meets our *despair*. I have no doubt that the two pathologies of denial and despair are broad and deep in our society and provide the matrix in which we do our preaching. I think the preacher must spend some time and energy in helping people acknowledge the denial we commonly practice (not least by euphemisms) and the despair we embrace without naming it.

If that double diagnosis of our common malady can be established, even amid what will no doubt be great resistance, then the preacher can celebrate the church, the local congregation, as the only place in town where truth can be told that breaks the bubble of denial and hope can be told that shatters despair. The sermon series could seek to make the case that the church is an odd place, but that is why we come, because we talk differently about different themes. Clearly we do so because we are in touch with ancient words (ancient bones) that are not generated by current self-deceptions. Thus the series from the randomly selected texts:

Amos 7:7–14. God's truth, as best we have access to it, is "inconvenient." The text is a model for inconvenient utterance. We are invited to play both roles, the speaker and the resister, because the topic is the ominous reality of "dislocation" (exile).

Micah 5:21–5. This text makes a nice counterpoint to the Amos text. That text is about expose; this text is about a new gift of leadership that can enact well-being. The coming of "messiah" for the little village makes no sense, unless it is in the context of deep dislocation, the very kind now widely known among us.

Zephaniah 3:14–20. This text builds nicely from Micah 5 and imagines the effective impact of God's good coming. The news is that every system of domination, the ones we resist and the ones from which we benefit, are quite fleeting and penultimate; we in faith wait for that beyond the system that God will give because we know that the dominant system cannot deliver on its promises to us.

Isaiah 35:4–7. This text goes further and imagines a society of compassion in which the "disabled and the vulnerable" are placed in the center of the new social vision and the new social practice that God will initiate.

Isaiah 50:4–9. This poem offers a retrospective on what hard work such teaching and preaching is. It is hard work in the church because the church in our culture has become so "friendly" and "therapeutic" that the church unwittingly colludes with dominant culture and forms a "cocoon of pretend" that does not rush to the deep issues of power in the service of death.

Obviously such a sermon series would, in most congregations, offer ways of talking, thinking, and preaching that seem odd, intrusive, and unwelcome. That, however, is what happens when we touch the old bones and attend to the old words. Such a testimony leads, as did the ancient encounter, to "coming to life and standing up." Without such radioactive contact, there will be no "coming to life" and no "standing up." There will most often be only settling into the deathliness of denial and despair, only reclining in exhausted apathy.

VI.

In pondering the bones of Elisha, it becomes clear that the old prophetic legacy from a particular time and place continues to be generative. As we touch the old words, the old bones (spine) of ancient utterance, we may get energy for present utterance. We do not know what happened to the guy who touched the bones and "came to life and stood on his feet." But we may imagine that he was somebody like John Holbert. Given his new radioactive energy, he went on out to truth-telling. We may imagine that he did it effectively, like John, with grace and humor and deep caring. His name is "Legion," and John himself is a marvelous example of what happens when we touch old bones and hear old words, receiving freedom, imagination, and courage for our own proper work.

Notes

Chapter 1: You Can't Say That ! Preaching Jonah as Comedy

1   I am told that African scholars find it amusing when Westerners boast of where and with whom they have studied, recognizing that a far better indication of a scholar's worth is the quality of her or his students. I do not know John Holbert personally, but I admire his work, and more importantly, I know the quality of the people he has taught (including the editors of this volume)! I count myself privileged, then, to contribute to this book in his honor.

2   Bernhard W. Anderson, *Understanding the Old Testament*, Fourth Edition (Englewood Cliffs, NJ: Prentice-Hall, 19 6), 606–607.

3   Ibid., 607.

4   Millar Burrows also observes this problem; cf. "The Literary Category of the Book of Jonah," in *Translating and Understanding the Old Testament: Essays in Honor of Herbert Gordon May*, ed. Harry Thomas Frank and William L. Reed (Nashville: Abingdon Press, 1970), 95.

5   Unless otherwise noted, all Scripture quotes in this chapter are from the NRSV.

6   Frederick Buechner, *Telling the Truth: The Gospel as Tragedy, Comedy, and Fairy Tale* (San Francisco: Harper and Row, 1977), 66.

7   Brevard Childs, *Introduction to the Old Testament as Scripture* (Philadelphia: Fortress Press, 1979), 421–422; 426; and cf. James D. Smart, "Jonah: Introduction and Exegesis," in *The Interpreters Bible*, Volume VI, ed. G. A. Buttrick et al. (Nashville: Abingdon Press, 1956), 872–873. Similarly, Elizabeth Achtemeier calls Jonah a "didactic story" (*Minor Prophets I*, New International Biblical Commentary 17 [Peabody, MA: Hendrickson, 1996], 258). Cf. also the discussions of the history of the interpretation of Jonah in Burrows, "Literary Category," 88–92, and Jack M. Sasson, *Jonah*, Anchor Bible 24B (New York: Doubleday, 1990), especially 334–337.

8   E.g., John C. Holbert, who more precisely classifies Jonah as "a short story characterized by the use of satire" ("'Deliverance Belongs to

133

Yahweh': Satire in the Book of Jonah," *Journal for the Study of the Old Testament* 21 [1981]: 60); Burrows, who calls Jonah a satire ("Literary Category," 94–97, 105); and Jack M. Sasson, who describes Jonah as a "comic hero" (*Jonah*). Lawrence Wood writes, "The book of Jonah is structured like a joke" ("Jonah 3:1–5, 10: Homiletical Perspective," in *Feasting on the Word: Year B, Volume 1*, ed. David L. Bartlett and Barbara Brown Taylor [Louisville: Westminster John Knox Press, 2008], 267); his homiletical observations throughout this article explore the humor in Jonah. Richard Boyce, who says that "Jonah is difficult to classify," nonetheless observes regarding Nineveh in this book, "One of the favorite jokes of the Scriptures is the unexpected faithfulness of the outsider, the other, the enemy" ("Jonah 3:1–5, 10: Exegetical Perspective," *Feasting on the Word: Year B, Volume 1*, 267). Phyllis Trible prefers to permit Jonah to move freely among the genres of folktale, parable, satire, and midrash ("The Book of Jonah: Introduction, Commentary, and Reflections," in *The New Interpreter's Bible* [*NIB*], Volume 7, ed. Leander Keck [Nashville: Abingdon Press, 1996], 466–474).

9 Robert K. Gnuse, *The Old Testament and Process Theology* (St. Louis: Chalice Press, 2000), 128.

10 Burrows, "Literary Category," 93. Cf. also Holbert, "Satire," 64.

11 The older version of the NIV rationalized this exaggeration by means of a dubious paraphrase: "a visit required three days." Thankfully, this has been corrected in the 2011 edition, which reads, "it took three days to go through it."

12 E.g., the KJV, the NRSV, the NIV, and the NJPS.

13 *HALOT* 1: 51. Possible examples listed are Gen. 23:6 and 1 Sam. 14:15, where the NRSV translates *'elohim* as the superlative, and Gen. 1:2 and Job 1:16, where it does not.

14 Trible, "Jonah," 511.

15 With Timothy B. Cargal: "Any homiletical appropriation of the book of Jonah that does not take into account the humor so skillfully interwoven into the story has missed both a key aspect of its literary character and a useful rhetorical opportunity" ("Jonah 3:10–4:11: Homiletical Perspective," in *Feasting on the Word: Year A, Volume 4*, ed. David L. Bartlett and Barbara Brown Taylor [Louisville: Westminster John Knox Press, 2011], 75).

16 Thomas Paine, *Age of Reason,* Part II, Section 13 (http://www.ushistory. org/paine/reason/singlehtml.htm); cf. Sasson, 324; Burrows, 95. Similarly, though without Paine's anti-biblical polemic, Holbert characterizes Jonah as "an attack on prophetic hypocrisy" (Holbert, "Satire," 75).

17 Smart, "Jonah," 872. This reading goes back at least to Wellhausen in the late nineteenth century, who wrote that Jonah is "directed against

the impatience of the Jewish believers, who are fretted because, notwithstanding all predictions, the antitheocratic world-empire has not yet been destroyed" (cited by Sasson, 324).

18 Northrop Frye, *Anatomy of Criticism* (Princeton: Princeton University, 1967), 224.

19 As Holbert observes, "Satire has a definite target which must be familiar enough to make the assault meaningful and memorable" ("Satire," 62).

20 Clements, Robert E. "The Purpose of the Book of Jonah," in *Congress Volume: Edinburgh 1974*, ed. G. W. Anderson et al.; SuppVT 28 (Leiden: E. J. Brill, 1975), 27.

21 Ibid.

22 Cf. Beate Ego, "The Repentance of Nineveh in the Story of Jonah and Nahum's Prophecy of the City's Destruction–A Coherent Reading of the Book of the Twelve as Reflected in the Aggadah," in *Thematic Threads in the Book of the Twelve*, ed. Aaron Schart and Paul L. Redditt; BZAW 325 (Berlin: de Gruyter, 2003), 159.

23 Cf. Ehud ben Zvi, "Introduction and Notes on Jonah," in *The Jewish Study Bible*, ed. Adele Berlin and Marc Zvi Brettler (New York: Oxford University, 2004), 1199.

24 Note that this list follows the order of the Twelve, or the Minor Prophets, from the Septuagint (LXX), the Greek translation of Jewish Scripture, rather than the order from the Hebrew Masoretic Text (MT) that is also reflected in our Old Testament.

25 Accordingly, many early and pre-critical Christian interpreters read Jonah as a type for Christ. So Tertullian wrote that Jonah "would have been lost, were it not for the fact that what he endured was a type of the Lord's suffering, by which pagan penitents also would be redeemed" (*On Purity* 10; cited in *Ancient Christian Commentary on Scripture, Old Testament XIV: The Twelve Prophets*, ed. Albert Ferreiro [Downers Grove, IL: InterVarsity, 2003], 134), and John Calvin concluded, "Hence Jonah was not a type of Christ, because he was sent away unto the Gentiles, but because he returned to life again, after having for some time exercised his office as a Prophet among the people of Israel" (*Commentary on Jonah*, Lecture 72, in *Commentaries on the Twelve Minor Prophets*, trans. John Owen [Grand Rapids, MI: Christian Classics Ethereal Library, 2005 {orig. Edinburgh: Calvin Translation Society,1847}], http://www.ccel.org/ccel/calvin/calcom28.iii.1.ii.html.)

26 Cf. Cyril of Jerusalem, *Catecheses* XIV.17.

27 While the MT of Jonah 1:4 reads *ru'ach gedolah* ("a great wind"), the LXX has only *pneuma* ("wind"). Intriguingly, none of the Synoptics follows the LXX here. Matt. 8:24 has *seismos megas* (literally, "a great shaking"), Mark 4:37 has *lailaps megale* ("a great windstorm"), Luke 8:23 has simply *lailaps* ("a windstorm").

28 The NRSV of Jonah 1:5 puts the prophet in "the hold of the ship"; MT has *yarkete hassepinah*, that is, the bottom or the back of the ship; the LXX reads *ten koilen tou ploiou*, that is, the hollow of the ship. Mark 4:38 specifies that Jesus was asleep *en te prumne*: in the stern, or the back, of the boat.

29 Jonah 1:15 says "the sea ceased from its raging" (MT *wayya'amod hayyam mizza'po*; the LXX renders this faithfully). In Matt. 8:26 and Mark 4:39, there is "a great calm" (*palene megale*); in Luke 8:24, "a calm" (*palene*).

30 Buechner, *Telling the Truth*, 57. Cf. also John Holbert's sermon, "The Best Laugh of All," in his *Preaching Old Testament: Proclamation and Narrative in the Hebrew Bible* (Nashville: Abingdon Press, 1991), 79–92, especially 81.

31 Ibid.

32 Northrop Frye, *The Great Code: The Bible and Literature* (San Diego: Harcourt Brace Jovanovich, 1982), 169.

33 Abraham J. Heschel, *The Prophets*, Vol. 2 (New York: Harper & Row, 1975), 67.

34 *Contra* Holbert, "Satire," 70–75. For Jonah 2:2–9 (3–10) as an originally independent psalm secondarily incorporated into its context, cf. James Nogalski, *Redactional Processes in the Book of the Twelve*, BZAW 218 (Berlin: de Gruyter, 1993), 265; and Trible, 464–465. Jack Sasson, who like Holbert reads Jonah 2:2–9 (3–10) in continuity with the prose of Jonah, nonetheless recognizes its distinctiveness, and does not claim that it was composed for its place in the book (Sasson, 165). For other examples of a song secondarily incorporated into a book, whether by its author or by its editors, cf. Isa 2:1–4//Mic. 4:1–3; Nah. 1:2–11; Hab. 3; and in the NT, Phil. 2:6–11.

35 Childs, *Introduction*, 422–425.

36 As Gregory of Nazianzus proposed; cf. *Orat* II:106.

37 So Daniel C. Timmer, "God and Nineveh, Jonah and Nahum: Odd Pairs and Coherence in the Twelve." Presented at the annual meeting of the Society of Biblical Literature, November 22, 2010, in Atlanta, GA.

38 Some scholars date the composition of Nahum, in part or in whole, to soon after the fall of Thebes in 663 B.C.E., described in Nah. 3:8–10: e.g., Klaas Spronk, *Nahum*, HCOT (Kampen: Kok Pharos, 1997); J.J.M. Roberts, *Nahum, Habakkuk, and Zephaniah*, OTL (Louisville: Westminster/John Knox Press, 1991). However, one might question whether the gloating, mocking tone of Nah. 3:1–7, or 3:18–19, would have been possible in a time of Assyrian strength. It makes more sense to date this poetry closer to the time of Nineveh's destruction, when Assyria was in decline, or even shortly after the city's fall in 612 B.C.E.; so Steven Tuell, "Nahum," in *The Lexham Bible Dictionary* (Bellingham, WA: Logos, 2011) http://www.lexhambibledictionary.com/, and

Marvin Sweeney, *The Twelve Prophets*, Vol. 2; Berit Olam (Collegeville, MN: Liturgical Press, 2000), 422.

39 Clement ("Purpose," 28) dates Jonah to the late sixth century, while Nogalski (*Redactional Processes*, 272) holds rather for a date in the third century. Based on Jonah's literary and linguistic features, Sasson (26–27) is willing to state that the book was assembled in "the post-exilic period," but doubts that we can say much more than that. 4QXIIa, a fragment of the Book of the Twelve from Qumran, places Jonah at the end of the Twelve, following Malachi, which likely reflects its late composition.

40 For a fine treatment of the Twelve as a book, cf. *Interpretation* 61 (2007), which was devoted to the Book of the Twelve, and in particular Jim Nogalski, "Recurring Themes in the Book of the Twelve: Creating Points of Contact for a Theological Reading," *Interpretation* 61 (2007): 125–137. For a critique of this perspective, cf. Ehud ben Zvi, "Twelve Prophetic Books or 'The Twelve': A Few Preliminary Considerations," in *Forming Prophetic Literature: Essays on Isaiah and the Twelve in Honor of John D. W. Watts*, ed. James W. Watts and Paul R. House; JSOTSupp 235 (Sheffield: Sheffield Academic, 1996), 125–156.

41 In the MT, as in our Old Testament, Micah comes between Jonah and Nahum, while in the LXX, Jonah immediately precedes Nahum. *The Martydom and Ascension of Isaiah* 4:22 places Nahum before Jonah, but its order is clearly idiosyncratic. 4QXIIa, as has already been observed, places Jonah at the end of the Book of the Twelve, after Malachi. But where the fragments of the Book of the Twelve from Cave Four preserve a sequence (the end of one book followed by the beginning of another), they generally support the MT: 4QXIIa has Zechariah followed by Malachi (though Malachi is followed by Jonah), 4QXIIb has Zephaniah followed by Haggai, and 4QXIIg has Nahum followed by Habakkuk (as well as Amos followed by Obadiah). This suggests that only Jonah may be out of place, likely placed last in 4QXIIa in accordance with its late composition, rather than its eighth-century setting (cf. 2 Kgs. 14:25).

42 Theodoret of Cyrus, *Commentary on the Twelve Prophets*, trans. Robert Charles Hill (Brookline: Holy Cross, 2006), 179; cf. also 177–178.

43 Cf. Ego, "The Repentance of Nineveh," 161–162.

44 John Calvin, *Commentary on Jonah*, Lecture 72.

45 Nogalski, *Redactional Processes*, 271. Indeed, Nogalski proposes that Jonah found a home among the Twelve for this very reason: "The narrative was selected as a contrast to the views of Nahum, whose bitter denunciation of Nineveh (within the context of cosmic judgment) leaves no room for YHWH's salvific action among the nations" (*Redactional Processes*, 270–271).

46 The articles on Jonah 3:1–5, 10 in *Feasting on the Word: Year B, Volume 1*, 267–271 by Richard Boyce ("Exegetical Perspective") and Lawrence

Wood ("Homiletical Perspective") are particularly useful for their focus on the humor in this passage.

47 Cf. Smart, "Jonah," 872; Wood, "Homiletical Perspective," 271.

48 Cf. *Feasting on the Word: Year A, Volume 4,* 74–79, particularly the articles by Timothy B. Cargal ("Homiletical Perspectives") and Todd M. Hobbie ("Pastoral Perspectives").

49 *The Revised Common Lectionary,* The Consultation on Common Texts (Nashville: Abingdon Press, 1992), 18–19.

50 The JPSV renders *khus* here as "care for."

51 Heschel, *The Prophets,* 67. Cf. Boyce: "Maybe the main joke and gospel in this strange book of Jonah is the sense that not even the Lord knows how far divine mercy and compassion can go" ("Exegetical Perspective," 271.

52 The bracketing function is more evident in the MT, where these two verses introduce Jonah 2, than in our English Bibles, where the first verse closes Jonah 1, and the second opens Jonah 2.

53 Cf. *John Wesley,* ed. Albert C. Outler; Library of Protestant Thought (New York: Oxford University, 1964), 365–366.

54 E.g., the persistent–and false–claim that the Obama White House insists its tree be referred to as a "holiday" tree (cf. http://www.snopes.com/politics/christmas/ornaments.asp).

55 Frye, *The Great Code,* 169.

Chapter 2: Being Sent to the Principal's Office

1 I join many other preachers in trying not to refer to the two parts of the Bible as the Old and New Testaments because of the danger of supersessionism. In this chapter, I frequently employ a designation adapted from a Jewish way of referring to their Bible as TANAKH–Torah, Neveeim, and Ketuvim: Torah, Prophets, Writings. To these I add Gospels and Letters. This way of speaking implies continuity among the five parts of the Protestant Bible while acknowledging that the different parts have different contents. See Ronald J. Allen, "A New Name for the Old Book: Torah, Prophets, Writings, Gospels, Letters," *Encounter* 68 (2007), 53–62.

2 For the trajectories, see John C. Holbert and Ronald J. Allen, *Holy Root, Holy Branches: Christian Preaching from the Old Testament* (Nashville: Abingdon Press, 1995), 38–58.

3 Marjorie Suchocki uses the phrase "inclusive well-being" to describe God's purposes in her *The Fall to Violence: Original Sin in Relational Theology* (New York: Continuum International Publishing Group, 1994), 66.

4 The only parts of the Torah, Prophets, and Writings that are proto-apocalyptic or apocalyptic are Isaiah 56–66, Zechariah 9–14, and

Daniel 7–12. In addition, the apocalyptic perspective is found in
2 Esdras (4 Ezra) and many other documents in the Pseudepigrapha.

5 This word is sometimes transliterated *chesed* or *khesed.*

6 For a summary of Sakenfeld's voluminous writings on *hesed:* "Love in
the OT" in *The New Interpreter's Bible,* ed. Katherine D. Sakenfeld et al.
(Nashville: Abingdon Press, 2008), vol. 3, 713–718.

7 Katherine D. Sakenfeld, *Faithfulness in Action: Loyalty in Biblical
Perspective,* Overtures to Biblical Theology (Philadelphia: Fortress Press,
1985), 39–82; cf. her earlier *The Meaning of Hesed in the Hebrew Bible,*
SBL Dissertation Series (Missoula: Scholars Press, 1978).

8 Sakenfeld, *Faithfulness in Action,* 40.

9 For the relationship between promise and law in covenant, see John C.
Holbert, *The Ten Commandments. The Great Texts: A Preaching Commentary*
(Nashville: Abingdon Press, 2002).

10 Later thinkers expanded these themes, e.g. Jubilees 7:20–28 and b.
Sanhedrin 56b.

11 Although people today sometimes speak of any suffering as "hell on
earth," in the apocalyptic tradition hell was intended to cause the wicked
to suffer.

12 Ancient people often conceived of blessing and curse in communal
terms because they thought of identity as communal. While it might
seem to us unfair for people who did not actually violate the covenant
to be punished for a violation, ancients would have typically regarded
such a phenomenon as consistent with communal identity.

13 Translated by E. Isaac, "1 Enoch," in *The Old Testament Pseudepigrapha*
ed. James H. Charlesworth (Garden City: Doubleday & Company,
1983), vol. 1.

14 For an invigorating treatment of Job, see John C. Holbert, *Preaching
Job: Preaching Classic Texts* (St. Louis: Chalice Press, 1999).

15 See Paul D. Hanson, *The Dawn of Apocalyptic: The Historical and
Sociological Roots of Jewish Apocalyptic Eschatology,* rev. ed. (Philadelphia:
Fortress Press, 1979), 161–185.

16 On sermon series, see Ronald J. Allen, *Preaching is Believing: The Sermon
as Theological Reflection* (Louisville: Westminster John Knox Press, 2002),
107–112.

17 On topical preaching, see Ronald J. Allen, *Preaching the Topical Sermon*
(Louisville: Westminster John Knox Press, 1992).

Chapter 3: It Seemed Like a Good Idea at the Time

1 See Richard B. Wilke, *Disciple: Becoming Disciples Through Bible Study*
(Nashville, TN: Abingdon Press, 1993).

2 An "emotional triangle" is formed in response to stress between
two people or parts of a system. In order to relieve the stress of a
relationship, one or both of the two parties "triangle in" a third person

or party. While triangling can be a healthy way to relieve tension if the third party is skilled in staying neutral yet connected to both parties, it can also result in some unhealthy situations. Those who work in the church will recognize the kind of situation I am talking about: Two members of the congregation are having a dispute and want the pastor to decide between them. Sometimes the attempt to triangle is obvious and sometimes subtle but always needs to be recognized. For a much more complete explanation of emotional triangles and the part they play in Family Systems theory, see Edwin H. Friedman, *Generation to Generation: Family Process in Church and Synagogue*, (New York: The Guilford Press, 1985).

3   Friedman, 210–211.
4   Ibid., 41.

Chapter 4: Sexuality and Eroticism

1   David M. Carr, *The Erotic Word: Sexuality, Spirituality, and the Bible* (Oxford: Oxford University Press, 2003), 54.
2   Esther M. Menn, "Sexuality in the Old Testament: Strong as death, unquenchable as fire," *Currents in Theology and Mission* (February 2003).
3   The reasons why this is so clearly outlined in Ronald J. Allen and John C. Holbert, *Holy Root, Holy Branches: Christian Preaching From the Old Testament* (Nashville: Abingdon Press, 1995).
4   Laura Betzig, "Politics as Sex: The Old Testament Case," *Evolutionary Psychology*, vol. 3 (2005):326–346.
5   Ibid.
6   Ibid.
7   Ibid.
8   Current statistics regarding domestic violence found on domesticviolencestatistics. org:
   • Every nine seconds in the U.S. a woman is assaulted or beaten.
   • Around the world, at least one in every three women has been beaten, coerced into sex, or otherwise abused during her lifetime. Most often, the abuser is a member of her own family.
   • Domestic violence is the leading cause of injury to women–more than car accidents, muggings, and rapes combined.
   • Studies suggest that up to 10 million children witness some form of domestic violence annually.
   • Nearly one in five teenage girls who have been in a relationship said a boyfriend threatened violence or self-harm if presented with a breakup.
   • Every day in the U.S., more than three women are murdered by their husbands or boyfriends.
   • Ninety-two percent of women surveyed listed reducing domestic violence and sexual assault as their top concern.

9   For a theological discussion about the issues of sexual and domestic abuse, the role of the preacher to name and address these issues and model sermons, see John S. McClure and Nancy J. Ramsay, eds., *Telling the Truth: Preaching Against Sexual and Domestic Violence* (United Church Press, 1998). See also Mary Donovan Turner, "Lenten Light: Domestic Violence and Preaching," in *Journal for Preachers,* Volume XXX, No. 2, 22–27. In the latter, Turner addresses more fully domestic violence as a Lenten theme.

10   Turner, "Lenten Light," 25.

11   Carr, 5.

12   Ibid., 6.

13   Ibid., 7.

14   Audre Lorde, "The Uses of the Erotic: The Erotic as Power," in her *Sister Outsider: Essays and Speeches* (Freedom, CA: Crossing, 1984), 56, as found in Carr, 9.

15   As an eloquent example by a master preacher, see the sermon "The Two Loves," by Frederick Buechner in *The Hungering Dark* (San Francisco, CA: Harper and Row, 1969), 81–89.

16   Carr, 10.

17   The depiction of the relationship between God and Israel as man and woman or husband and wife is common in the Old Testament prophetic literature. Often the male/female relationship is used to depict a God/human relationship gone awry, where there has been unfaithfulness on the part of the community, where there is hurt and betrayal and anger and judgment (see Hos. 1–2, Isa. 49, etc.). Carr indicates that this image of God in relation to the female Israel, where God is depicted as a passionate, jealous, vengeful husband and Israel as God's battered wife, is a reminder that our notions of God are permeated with patriarchy. It counters our tendency to romanticize *eros,* and teaches us about idolatry, which is love gone awry.
It is interesting that the very "to know" in Hebrew is used to name human intercourse and also the kind of relationship we yearn for with God–we long "to know" God.

18   Carr, 143. In his volume *The Erotic Word,* Carr delineates the history of interpretation in Song of Songs in a detailed and helpful fashion. His complete analysis could not be represented here.

19   Ibid., 143–144.

20   Ibid., 144–146.

21   Juan and Stacey Floyd-Thomas, "Marriage Enrichment Sunday: Sunday, March 22, 2009," Africanamericanlectionary.org.

22   See Mary Tolbert's 2004 article "The Bible and Same Gender Marriage," (www.clgs.org), where she persuasively argues that this text is not about marriage; it is about relationship and sexuality. Thus, it cannot be used with integrity to argue for an exclusive, heterosexual

understanding of marriage. Found on the Center for Lesbian and Gay Studies, Berkeley, CA, website.

23 For a fuller explication of these verses in relation to time honored interpretations that denigrate woman and her place in society, see Phyllis Trible, *God and the Rhetoric of Sexuality* (Philadelphia: Fortress Press, 1978), 94–105.

24 It is recognized that while the Song of Songs depicts a relationship between men and women that is fairly mutual and equitable, Qohelet is a man speaking to men about life and how to live it.

25 Ken Stone, *Practicing Safer Texts: Food, Sex, and Bible in Queer Perspective* (London and New York: T & T Clark International, 2005), 137.

26 Ibid.

Chapter 5: One Step Forward, Two Steps Back

1 Richard D. Nelson, *From Eden to Babel: An Adventure in Bible Study* (St. Louis: Chalice Press, 2006) 25–66.

2 The Hebrew Bible tends to blame the woman in situations of sexual transgression. The story of Joseph and Potiphar's wife sounds like a narrative illustration of Proverbs 7. However, this is not always the case (Gen. 34; 2 Sam. 11; 13:1–19). Certainly Proverbs cannot be accused of unmitigated misogyny (cf. 5:18–19; 12:4; 18:22; 19:14; 31:10–31).

3 He goes on to point out that certain Catholic writers understand sanctification properly while misunderstanding justification, concluding, "But it has pleased God to give the Methodists a full and clear knowledge of each...." "On God's Vineyard [Sermon 107]," *Works of John Wesley, Sermons III, 71–114* (Nashville: Abingdon Press, 1986), 505–506.

4 The *ummanu* were post-Flood scribes who transmitted cultural knowledge to humanity. Richard Clifford, *Proverbs: A Commentary* (Louisville: Westminster John Knox Press), 24–27, 99–101.

5 The regular and semi-continuous lections for Year B of the Revised Common Lectionary offer a cluster of Proverbs texts that could serve as the core of a ready-made mid-August and September series: Proper 15 (9:1–6), Proper 18 (selected verses from chapter 22), Proper 19 (1:20–33), and Proper 20 (31:10–31). The themes of these texts would fit the annual restart of programming and education. Except for the last, all these texts address the problem of the "simple" (1:22, 32; 9:4, 6; 22:3).

Chapter 6: Body/Parts: Body Image in the Old Testament

1 "Arqu," *Chicago Assyrian Dictionary* (Chicago: Oriental Institute, 1968) I:2, 300301.

2 James Barr has cautioned about being led astray through etymological arguments from silence (*Comparative Philology and the Text of the Old*

Testament [Winona Lake, IN: Eisenbrauns, 2001], 223–27). Since a literary corpus like the Bible is a relatively limited selection of texts, Hebrew as the living language that people spoke in ancient Israel encompassed a much larger vocabulary than what we find in the Bible. Simply because a word never appears in the Hebrew text of the Bible does not mean that ancient people did not use it either in everyday life or in highly specialized contexts. This applies, of course, to words for specific things or actions that occur in contexts outside of those alluded to or represented in the Bible. Some phenomena, however, seem to be universal; they occur in almost every context. "Yellow," it seems to me, is one of these phenomena; "human body" is another.

3 R. Eduard Schweizer, "Body," *ABD* I:767–72.

4 Joel B. Green, "Body," *NIDB* I:483–85.

5 According to the *Oxford English Dictionary*, a "body" in this sense is the "complete physical form of a person or animal; the assemblage of parts, organs, and tissues that constitutes the whole material organism" (*s.v.*). While the Old Testament clearly has words for the "parts, organs, and tissues" that constitute a physical person, there is no word that designates the "complete physical form of a...whole material organism." In other words, there is no word for "body."

6 The word "body"/"bodies" occurs 128 times in 116 verses in the Old Testament texts of the NRSV.

7 Gen. 47:18; Jdg. 14:8f; 1 Sam. 31:10, 12 (twice); Neh. 9:37; Ps. 110:6; Ezek. 1:11, 23; Dan. 10:6; Nah. 3:3 (twice).

8 In this discussion, I have left out Ezek. 1:11, 23 and Dan. 10:6 because those passages do not deal with "human" bodies, but rather the physical appearances of supernatural beings.

9 Probably a reference to her pubic area. Roland Murphy sees verse 6 as a problem, since it "interrupts the description of the woman, which ends in 4:7" (*Song of Songs* [Hermeneia; Minneapolis: Fortress Press, 1990], 155). If my supposition is correct, the verse does not interrupt the poem, but rather the poem as a whole finds its climax in this verse. Interestingly, Marvin Pope, who is certainly no prude in his commentary, seems to ignore the ordering of the parts and interprets the verse as referring to the woman's breasts instead of her vulva. See *Song of Songs* (Anchor Bible; New York: Doubleday, 1977), 472.

10 One wonders if, in this line, the reference to the "appearance" is a euphemism for penis, since it would follow in the order downward: head, hair, eyes, cheeks, lips, arms, torso, leg (more exactly, "upper thigh"), and "appearance." Furthermore, if this is what is meant, the comparison with a cedar of Lebanon would be appropriate.

11 See note 5.

12 Schweizer, "Body," I:768.

13 Green, "Body," I:484.

14 Literally, "When I was silent, my bones wore out...."
15 The Hebrew text of the second half of verse 4 is completely corrupt. In the wider sense of the psalm as a whole, it seems clear that the line is the climax of the horrors the psalmist endures while not acknowledging his/her sin.
16 From verse 6 forward, the poetic organization and meter of the psalm is inconsistent.
17 The Hebrew word here, *remiyyah*, seems to reflect things that are not as they seem to be, and therefore are dangerous. See Hos. 7:16; Ps. 78:57; 120: 2, 3.
18 The verb *sha'ag* is translated in the NRSV as "groaning," but always refers to the roar of a lion (Isa. 5:29; Ezek. 19:7; Zech. 11:3; Job 4:10) or the scream of someone in pain or despair (Ps. 22:2; Job 3:24). I believe that its use is meant to contrast with the idea of "being silent" in verse 3. No matter if the psalmist was silent or screaming, as long as his sin is unknown or unacknowledged the result was the same.
19 In Hebrew, the sentence has only six words!
20 Of course, there will be those in the congregation who are not able to use and have some senses. The sermon should be thought about and written and preached in such a way that those without sight or hearing might know that all "seeing" is not done through the eyes and those who are deaf can often "hear" better than those "with ears"!
21 Lev. 1:9, 13, 17; 2:2, 9, 12; 3:5, 16; 4:31; 6:8, 14; 8:21, 28; 17:6; 23:13, 18; 26:31; Num. 15:3, 7, 10, 13–14, 24; 18:17; 28:2, 6, 8, 13, 24, 27; 29:2, 6, 8, 13, 36.
22 Note the discussion of Exod. 17:1–7 above.

Chapter 7: Moses Meets Main Street

1   Bernard Brandon Scott, *Hollywood Dreams and Biblical Stories* (Minneapolis: Fortress Press, 1994), 11.
2   John C. Lyden, *Film as Religion: Mythos, Morals, and Rituals* (New York: New York University Press, 2003), 2.
3   Ibid., 3–4.
4   Adele Reinhartz, *Scripture on the Silver Screen* (Louisville: Westminster John Knox Press, 2003), 188.
5   Robert K. Johnston, "Introduction: Reframing the Discussion," in *Reframing Theology and Film: New Focus for an Emerging Discipline*, ed. Robert K. Johnston (Grand Rapids, MI: Baker Academic, 2007) 16.
6   Clive Marsh, "On Dealing with What Films Actually Do to People: The Practice and Theory of Film Watching in Theology/Religion and Film Discussion," in *Reframing Theology and Film: New Focus for an Emerging Discipline*, ed. Robert K. Johnston (Grand Rapids, MI: Baker Academic, 2007), 150.
7   Johnston, *Reel Spirituality*, 13.

8   Scott, 4.
9   Robert H. Woods Jr. and Paul D. Patton, *Prophetically Incorrect: A Christian Introduction to Media Criticism* (Grand Rapids, MI: Brazos Press, 2010), 44–45.
10 Michael Warren, *Seeing through the Media* (Harrisburg, PA: Trinity Press International, 1997), 158.
11 Gordon Lynch, "Film and the Subjective Turn: How the Sociology of Religion Can Contribute to Theological Readings of Film," in *Reframing Theology and Film: New Focus for an Emerging Discipline*, ed. Robert K. Johnston (Grand Rapids, MI: Baker Academic, 2007), 112.
12 Ibid.
13 Lyden, 2.
14 Scott, 16.
15 Woods and Patton, 53.
16 For an updating of this scheme as applied to preaching, see Paul Scott Wilson, *God Sense: Reading the Bible for Preaching* (Nashville: Abingdon Press, 2001).
17 Marshall McLuhan, *Understanding Media,* 2nd edition (New York: New American Library, 1964).
18 Guerric DeBona, *Film Adaptation in the Hollywood Studio Era* (Urbana: University of Ilinois Press, 2010), 29.
19 Ibid., 35
20 Lynch, 121.
21 Craig Detweiler, "Seeing and Believing: Film Theory as a Window into Visual Faith," in *Reframing Theology and Film: New Focus for an Emerging Discipline*, ed. Robert K. Johnston (Grand Rapids, MI: Baker Academic, 2007), 40.
22 Guerric DeBona, *Fulfilled in Our Hearing* (Mahweh, NJ: Paulist Press, 2005), 192.
23 DeBona, *Film Adaptation*, 23.
24 Walter Brueggemann, *Reverberations of Faith: A Theological Handbook of Old Testament Themes* (Louisville: Westminster John Knox Press, 2002).
25 Reinhartz, 5.
26 J. Cheryl Exum, "Do You Feel Comforted? M Shyamalan's *Signs* and the Book of Job," in *Foster Biblical Scholarships: Essays in Honor of Kent Harold Richards* (Atlanta: SBL, 2010), 251–267.
27 Douglas E. Cowan, *Sacred Space: The Quest for Transcendence in Science Fiction Film and Television* (Waco: Baylor University Press, 2010), 246–247.
28 David Buttrick, *Homiletic: Moves and Structures* (Philadelphia: Fortress Press, 1987), 293–301. See also Richard L. Eslinger's chapter on Buttrick in *A New Hearing: Living Options in Homiletic Method* (Nashville: Abingdon Press, 1987) 133–171.

29   Guerric DeBona, "Preaching for the Plot," *New Theology Review*, 14, no. 1 (2001): 15.
30   David Jasper and Allen Smith, *Between Truth and Fiction: A Narrative Reader in Literature and Theology*, ed. David Jasper and Allen Smith (Waco: Baylor University Press, 2010), 102.
31   Timothy B. Cargal, *Hearing a Film, Seeing a Sermon: Preaching and Popular Movies* (Louisville: Westminster John Knox Press, 2007), 7.
32   Ibid., 47.
33   Ibid., 7.
34   Reinhartz, 188.

Chapter 8: Poets of the Word

1   Rowan Williams, *Grace and Necessity: Reflections on Art and Love* (Harrisburg, PA: Morehouse, 2005), 26.
2   Ibid., 149–150.
3   Ibid., 63.
4   Flannery O'Connor, *Mystery and Manners*, Sally and Robert Fitzgerald, eds. (New York: Farrar, Straus, & Giroux, 1969), 79.
5   Williams, 11.
6   O'Connor, 65.
7   Ibid., 75.
8   Williams, 49–51.
9   Nicholas Wolterstorff, *Art in Action: Toward a Christian Aesthetic* (Grand Rapids, MI: Eerdmans, 1980), 18.
10   Don Saliers, "Liturgical Aesthetics: The Travail of Christian Worship," in *Arts, Theology, and the Church: New Intersections*, ed. Kimberly Yates and Wilson Yates (Cleveland: The Pilgrim Press, 2005), 189.
11   Ibid., 194.
12   Anna Carter Florence, "Put Away Your Sword!" in *What's the Matter with Preaching Today?*, ed. Mike Graves (Lousiville: Westminster John Knox Press, 2004), 99.
13   O'Connor, 163.
14   Jeremy Begbie, *Voicing Creation's Praise: Toward a Theology of the Arts* (Edinburgh, Scotland: T & T Clark, 1991), 213.
15   Anna Akmatova, "Lot's Wife," trans. Richard Wilbur. Found in Wilbur's *New and Collected Poems* (New York: Harcourt Brace Jovanovich, 1989), 167.
16   Søren Kierkegaard, *Fear and Trembling*, trans. and ed. Howard V. Hong and Edna H. Hong (Princeton: Princeton University Press, 1983), 28–29.
17   This poem is cited in Robert Atwan and Laurance Wieder, eds., *Chapters into Verse: A Selection of Poetry in English Inspired by the Bible from Genesis Through Revelation* (New York: Oxford University Press, 2000), 51. This anthology contains a wide range of poems keyed to specific passages

of scripture, and is an extraordinarily helpful resource for preachers wishing to use poetry in sermons.

18 James Weldon Johnson, *God's Trombones: Seven Negro Sermons in Verse* (New York: The Viking Press, 1927), 17.

19 C. S. Lewis, *The Chronicles of Narnia: The Magician's Nephew* (New York: Collier Books, 1970), 99.

Chapter 9: The Living Afterlife of a Dead Prophet

1 See Claus Westermann, *Basic Forms of Prophetic Speech* (Philadelphia: Westminster Press, 1967).

2 See Erik Erikson, "The Problem of Ego Identity," *Idem., Identity and the Life Cycle* (New York: International Universities Press, 1959)101–164.

3 Abraham J. Heschel, *Who Is Man?*(Stanford: Stanford University Press, 1965)112–113.

4 Jonathan Glover, *Humanity: A Moral History of the Twentieth Century* (New Haven: Yale University Press, 1999) 353–354.

5 I refer to Ezekiel 37:1–14. "The Valley of Dry Bones" makes a nice counterpoint to the bones of Elisha in our text. In both cases, the wonderment is that the old, dead bones can live again…by the power of God.

6 See Claus Westermann, *Prophetic Oracles of Salvation in the Old Testament* (Louisville: Westminster John Knox Press, 19991).

7 Paul D. Hanson, "Israelite Religion in the Early Postexilic Period," *Ancient Israelite Religion: Essays in Honor of Frank Moore Cross,* ed. Patrick D. Miller, Jr., et al. (Philadelphia: Fortress Press, 1987)485–508.

8 The speech has been reprinted in many contexts. See "I Have a Dream," *Sociology of Religion: A Reader,* ed. Susanne C. Monahan et al. (Upper Saddle River, NJ: Prentice Hall, 2001) 404–406.

9 Bruce Feiler, *America's Prophet: Moses and the American Story* (New York: Harper Collins, 2009) 251–252.